FUTURE PROOF

ISBN: 979-8-9991842-0-7

Library of Congress Control Number: 2025914564

Published by Erin E. Malone
Book layout by Erin E. Malone
Cover design by Lori Green
Cover artwork by Erin E. Malone

First Edition, July 2025

This book is for informational purposes only and is not a substitute for professional advice. The author and publisher are not liable for any damages resulting from its use.

Visit the author's website at www.erinemalone.com

Future Proof:

The Intersection of Bitcoin and Longevity

Erin E. Malone

For the resilient, the forward-thinking, and those ready to shape their own future.

Table of Contents

Mining Rewards:

Collect Mining Rewards and Recipes Throughout This Book

Bitcoin miners earn rewards by investing energy and effort to secure the network. In the same spirit, as you read *Future Proof*, you'll discover "Mining Rewards" and "Recipes," actionable tips, tools, and insights I've personally found valuable for reclaiming your health, building lasting wealth, and proactively shaping your future.

Starting in Chapter 2, each chapter offers practical suggestions you can experiment with and adapt freely to your own journey. You don't need specialized knowledge or technical expertise. Just curiosity, openness, and a willingness to explore.

By the end of this book, you'll have gathered powerful resources to help you build resilient habits, pursue financial independence, and confidently navigate whatever the future holds.

Collect your Mining Rewards and explore these Recipes at your own pace. This is your journey.

Foreword:

We live in a world built on systems. These systems dictate how we should live. They tell us what's best for us, how to manage our money, when to go to the doctor, and even how to think. These systems are so ingrained in our DNA, so deeply wired into our brains, that we don't question them; instead, we simply follow the script. Whether it's our monetary system or our healthcare system, we accept them as the way things are.

We're taught to trust financial advisors with our savings, assuming they'll preserve our hard-earned wealth and secure our retirement. When it comes to our health, the system isn't designed to keep us well; it's built to treat us once we're already sick. We're taught to live reactively, not proactively, outsourcing our financial security and physical well-being to institutions that often work against us.

This book isn't financial or health advice. It's my personal philosophy, shaped by years immersed in the Bitcoin community, hosting meetups, and exploring the intersections of AI, health, and longevity. Over time, I've come to realize that real freedom, both financial and physical, comes from actively taking control of your future instead of relying on institutions that profit from keeping you dependent.

Time is our most precious asset, and Bitcoin is the perfect vehicle to preserve it, protecting your future from inflation and loss. My own journey has shown me the transformative power of mindset, discipline, and delayed gratification. These principles, reinforced by Bitcoin and proactive wellness, motivated me to invest meaningfully in both my financial future and physical well-being.

In these pages, I share insights, practical strategies, and personal experiences that have helped me forge a resilient path forward. By embracing a mindset of low time preference (choosing long-term gains over immediate pleasures), we reclaim our most valuable resource: time.

This is my story, a testament to what becomes possible when you intentionally invest in yourself. May these ideas inspire you to take back control, cultivate resilience, and build a future where your health and wealth thrive in harmony.

Part 1

Understanding the Systems Keeping You Trapped

Chapter 1

The Illusion of Security: Question Everything

A Childhood of Questions

I was four years old, lying awake, terrified that a single wrong thought could send me straight to hell. I grew up in a world afraid of questions, a place where curiosity felt dangerous and answers rarely went deeper than, "That's just how it is." Information was filtered carefully through someone else's beliefs. Don't ask questions. Don't challenge authority. Don't disrupt the way things are. One of my earliest memories is asking "Why?" and instantly feeling I'd crossed some invisible line.

Those early moments planted seeds that grew into a lifelong pursuit to understand why: why systems failed, why people suffered, and ultimately, why taking control of one's life mattered so deeply.

The Berlin Wall had just fallen. It was 1989, the year I came into the world. Globally, everything was shifting, yet my small corner of Eastern Ohio, at the edge of Appalachia, felt untouched by the ripples of change spreading across the world. Like many others in our town, I grew up below the poverty line. Our house was old and drafty, with gaps and cracks that let nature slip inside. Summers were thick with humidity, leaving everything sticky. Winters were frigid; I spent most of them shivering, the dry heat from our wood stove barely holding back the chill slipping through the walls. The house always smelled faintly of wood smoke and mildew, scents that never quite faded, no matter the season. I'd wake up to ladybugs crawling on my pillow or snakes wriggling their way through holes in the walls.

Growing up in the '90s, we didn't realize how drastically the world was about to change. It was the last childhood before the internet, when information meant dusting off an encyclopedia, reading the weekly paper, asking your neighbor, or opening the Bible.

My family survived on government handouts and free lunches at school. Money was a taboo topic. No one I knew had retirement savings or investments; money was something you earned, spent, and stressed over, not something you understood or invested for the future. There was a pervasive "work until you die" mentality, deeply ingrained from childhood. No one around me thought about building a future. Everything was rooted in the past, in what had always been. Never in what could be built.

Our town was conservative, religious, and rigid, especially for women. Unwritten rules governed our lives, dictating everything from our beliefs and behaviors to what was acceptable to question. Abuse was normalized. Everything was deeply rooted in religion and fear; at times, it felt undeniably cult-like. Through fourth grade, I attended the local Southern Baptist school, where our days revolved around chapel, warnings of hellfire, and strict teachings of creationism instead of science. Authority wasn't something you challenged; it was something you obeyed. Stepping out of line meant judgment, isolation, or worse.

Every morning began the same way: with pledges to the American flag, the Christian flag, and the Bible. We stood together chanting catechisms, reciting scripture, and listing books of the Bible like a rehearsed ritual. Obedience was absolute, questioning was dangerous, and punishment was swift. Teachers openly wielded a large wooden paddle, ready to enforce discipline without hesitation.

I vividly remember the day a *Teen Magazine* was discovered hidden in the girls' bathroom. Panic rippled through the classrooms as we were marched silently into chapel. The principal stood before us, eyes blazing, delivering a furious sermon, branding the magazine "filth" and "trash." His voice thundered, declaring that whoever brought or even read it was destined for hell. Silence filled the room. Whoever confessed would face immediate suspension. No one dared speak. We sat there, paralyzed by fear.

When *Harry Potter* arrived on bookshelves, it was swiftly banned for promoting witchcraft, which was another guaranteed path to eternal punishment. The message was unmistakable: stepping out of line, even in thought, risked severe consequences. Authority was absolute; critical thought was forbidden.

At home, this rigid power structure was mirrored. Men led, and women stayed quiet and submissive. Even as a child, deep down, something felt fundamentally wrong... unnatural, even though I lacked the words or context to articulate it.

Part of me wanted to believe this oppressive environment was simply an artifact of pre-internet isolation and ignorance. Yet, when I recently visited the school's website expecting sanitized language and softened messaging, I found it chillingly unchanged. The same rigid, frightening ideology stared back at me, still deeply rooted in fear and control. It read more like a cult manifesto than a school's philosophy. Every page reinforced the chilling message: Christian education isn't optional; it's "a mandate from God." True learning demands unquestioned obedience and occurs strictly in this order: "Control, Communication, Learning."

> "The Imperial need for control is so desperate because it is so unnatural."
>
> *- Star Wars, Andor*

Reflecting now, I realize these weren't isolated episodes; instead, they were symptoms of broader, deliberately engineered systems maintaining control through fear and dependency. It reminded me of that chilling line from *Star Wars*: "Fear will keep the local systems in line. Fear of this battle station." Like the Death Star, these systems were built to project strength, suppress dissent, and maintain obedience. But once you peer beneath their surface, their power is revealed as an illusion, a carefully maintained facade masking vulnerability and weakness. Control disguised as security.

My early confrontation with authoritarian control sparked an inner resistance that grew into a lifelong pursuit of autonomy, clarity, and truth. Breaking free from fear-based systems became the foundational step toward my self-directed sovereignty.

Repeating the Cycle

My immediate family was overweight or obese, as were most people in our town. It was a reality so widespread it was rarely questioned or even noticed. Eating was something you had to do, without giving much thought to what you ate. All that mattered was that it was cheap. The priority was cost, not quality. Despite growing up in a rural farming community, local produce was scarce. Everything we ate was imported, frozen, ultra-processed, and usually deep-fried. Health education didn't exist. We were relentlessly warned about the dangers of drugs and smoking, yet no one talked about the highly processed junk food we consumed daily. Sugar was an emotional currency. It wrapped itself around love, encouragement, and reward. After enduring Sunday church services, we'd be rewarded with donuts, a sugary consolation for hours spent on hard pews. Families typically stocked up on heavily sugared items like Mountain Dew, Lucky Charms, chips, and cookies, all affordable indulgences we relied on government aid to purchase.

During high school, I saw this up close while working at our town's only grocery store, where it wasn't unusual for 70% of all receipts to come from food stamps. Surrounded by farmland, our shelves were ironically filled with ultra-processed foods shipped from everywhere but Ohio. Making minimum wage, affording groceries from my own store was out of reach, so I'd scour the shelves looking for expired items I could sneak out for free. My favorite find was the outdated Tollhouse cookie dough.

Most of my coworkers had started working there at sixteen and never left. Now in their 40s and 50s, they quietly counted down the years until retirement, still stuck in the same job they'd begun as teenagers. As graduation approached, my manager pulled me aside, offering me a 50-cent-an-hour raise, bringing my wage to just $7.35 an hour, if I stayed on as assistant manager instead of leaving for college. Fifty cents! Gas alone was $4.20 a gallon at the time, meaning nearly the entire first hour of each workday would barely cover my commute. Why would I trade my future for that? His offer felt less like an opportunity and more like a warning of what my life could become if I didn't escape.

I felt a quiet, persistent hopelessness growing up there. People died young. Life followed a predictable script: graduate high school, go to church, get married, go to church, have kids, go to church, work until your body failed (usually in your 50s or 60s from heart disease, stroke, cancer, or diabetes) and, of course, go to church. Life was a loop of hardship and suffering, broken only by weekend tractor pulls. Even back then, I felt something was off. I didn't have the words for it, but I knew there had to be more than just surviving.

Yet even in that closed-off world, my grandmother quietly sparked my rebellion. Until I was twelve, she lived just down the road and took me to the library every week, letting me check out as many books as I could carry. She'd tell vivid stories about growing up in Boston and traveling to New York, always yearning to see more of the world. Sitting together in her living room chair, we'd watch National Geographic, exploring distant places. She encouraged the questions others dismissed, never tiring of my curiosity or shutting down my "whys." She was one of the only people who truly believed in me, always encouraging, always certain I could achieve anything I dreamed. She ignited a lifelong hunger for learning, convincing me that somewhere beyond our small town, a different kind of life was waiting.

The system I was born into didn't allow us to imagine life ten or twenty years down the line. There was no vision for the future, only the pressure of making it paycheck to paycheck, day by day. It didn't offer hope. It offered survival. Survival meant constant tradeoffs. Gas or groceries? Pay the bills or pay late fees? These weren't one-off emergencies; they were normal, just like knowing you'd better still make it to church on Sunday.

But I wanted more. I craved the freedom to forge a different path, paved not by survival and struggle, but by choice. I needed to see what else existed beyond those boundaries. I realized I wasn't safe; I was contained.

The only way out was to question everything. To learn the rules. And then, break them.

Breaking the Cycle

Determined to escape the confines of my childhood, I buried myself in work and academics, enrolling in college in 2008, right as the Great Financial Crisis took hold. Given my circumstances: the poverty I'd grown up in and the economy collapsing around me, college felt like the only viable path forward. I financed my education through a mix of scholarships, grants, and federal loans, all of which I was incredibly grateful to receive, since without money or credit, securing a personal loan was never an option. Even now, I'm baffled that anyone thought it was reasonable to let eighteen-year-olds borrow so much, or that college could possibly be that expensive in the first place. I vividly remember my first day in Econ 101, when the professor bluntly announced, "Welcome to college. The economy just collapsed. Good luck finding a job."

Undeterred, I hustled relentlessly. Coming from rock bottom, the only direction was upward. With no money for food, I'd wash dishes for friends, scraping dried pasta and hardened cheese off their dirty plates, trading clean pots and pans for their dining hall swipes. I'd sneak in Ziploc containers and fill them with whatever leftovers I could, stretching each meal as far as possible. Money was always scarce. When every calorie counted, nutrition became an afterthought; my sole focus was survival and success.

I participated in every project and internship available that didn't cost me money, gaining experience to bolster my resume. Throughout college, I worked two jobs while taking heavy course loads, strategically using my student loans to graduate early without sinking deeper into debt. Having money felt like my only ticket out of the system I was born into, a world built on poverty, struggle, and limitation. Driven by survival, I skipped meals, sacrificed sleep, ate whatever was free (usually junk food), and undermined my own health along the way.

During my junior year, I landed a transformative internship, becoming the traveling filmmaker for the crowned winner of the Miss Universe pageant. Based out of New York City, I traveled the world, expanding my horizons and experiencing diverse cultures and lifestyles. It was the first time I saw how different life could look outside the system I was raised in, but also the first time I encountered what real abject poverty looked like, traveling to places like India, the Dominican Republic, Panama, and Guatemala. That contrast stayed with me. I realized how limited my world had been, and how vast the spectrum of struggle was globally.

Yet even back in NYC, survival was still a struggle. My internship paid only $500 per month, while my dorm rent alone was $1,500. I shared a bathroom with fifty other girls and had to shower in the middle of the night to avoid waiting in line. I vividly remember being picked up in a limo, headed to JFK airport for Miss Universe trips, while eating peanut butter sandwiches in the backseat because I couldn't afford real meals. Sheer determination kept me going, knowing this experience was my best chance at securing a real job after graduation.

In the months leading up to graduation, I applied to over 500 jobs but received only one interview. One. I got the job and had just a week to get there. California felt like the ultimate escape, a fresh start thousands of miles away from everything familiar. With barely $200, I stuffed all my belongings into a worn-out VW Bug and headed west, guided only by printed MapQuest directions and a stack of 30-year-old Bon Jovi cassettes. The car had no air conditioning, windows that refused to roll down, and an engine that constantly overheated. Somehow, I made it.

I landed a role at a winery, working in multimedia and film production. I stayed there for about two years before eventually starting my own film production business. In my first year after college, I made more than both my parents combined, a whopping $48,000. It was enough to secure a tiny studio apartment, pay bills, and have a couple hundred dollars left over every month. Over the next five years, I worked hard to pay off my $40k student loan debt and began saving. Yet no matter how hard I worked and how much I saved, I felt like I was sprinting just to stay in place. The cost of living kept climbing: rent, groceries, gas, everything increased. Housing prices crept up faster than I could save, and owning a home felt more like a fantasy than a goal. I watched the banks get bailed out while people lost their homes and jobs. The system felt rigged, like living in a casino game where the rules were written by those at the top and the house always wins. The rest of us were just trying to survive long enough to play another round. The cost of living kept increasing, but the money in my pocket stayed the same.

Looking back, I realize I was operating with a **high time preference**, that is, chasing short-term wins even when they hurt me in the long run. Not because I wanted to, but because I never learned how to think long-term. It wasn't until later that I discovered the opposite approach: **low time preference,** or prioritizing long-term benefits over immediate gratification. The system taught me how to survive the day, not how to invest in the future.

When I turned twenty-three, my body began signaling distress. I developed severe dairy intolerance (after a childhood of mandatory milk with every meal) and numerous skin allergies, likely induced by work-related stress. My dietary awareness gradually improved, aided by California's abundant local produce and year-round good weather. Still, my diet wasn't perfect. Working in the wine industry meant my professional and social life revolved around wine, often surrounded by functioning alcoholics.

By early 2020, I was working harder and making more money than ever, but somehow it still felt like I couldn't get ahead. Like running full speed just to stand still. After six hard-earned years building my film production business, COVID erased an entire year's worth of projects overnight. Instability wasn't new. I'd spent the previous four years fleeing wildfires that scorched California wine country, evacuating each season as flames devoured wineries, vineyards, and homes. By the time the pandemic hit, uncertainty was already deeply embedded in my life.

As governments responded by printing trillions of dollars out of thin air, the system I'd grown up trusting suddenly felt fragile. Or maybe it always had been, and 2020 just exposed the cracks. Once I saw it, I couldn't unsee it. That uneasy feeling echoed exactly what I'd experienced watching the bank bailouts of 2008.

That's when Bitcoin finally clicked.

With my calendar suddenly empty, I had nothing but time, time I spent revisiting Bitcoin, which I'd first encountered in late 2017 during the chaotic ICO (initial coin offering) bubble. Back then, Bitcoin had seemed like just another speculative asset, lost among scams and hype. But now, Michael Saylor's insights offered something entirely different: a clear, compelling explanation of how money itself was fundamentally broken, and how Bitcoin could fix not only economics but countless underlying societal problems.

As Saylor described, "Bitcoin is a bank in cyberspace, run by incorruptible software, offering a global, affordable, simple, and secure savings account to billions of people." He also called Bitcoin "the world's first 'perfect money,'" a currency that cannot be devalued, censored, or manipulated. That idea resonated deeply with me.

I became obsessed, spending ten, twelve, sometimes fifteen hours a day consuming podcasts, articles, books, really everything I could find. The deeper I went, the broader Bitcoin's implications became, touching philosophy, history, energy, and human rights. Bitcoin was more than magic internet money. It became a framework that explained why so many systems around me had failed. It provided clarity amidst chaos, grounding me when the world felt completely adrift.

It felt like waking up. I realized I hadn't understood money at all. Our monetary system is intentionally designed to keep people trapped on a hamster wheel their entire lives: work harder, run faster, die.

Digging into the history of money, one painful pattern repeated itself: every time a government, king, or ruler manipulated the currency, that money, and eventually the civilization built around it, collapsed. Every single time. The more I learned, the clearer it became: broken money was at the root of economic, social, and even personal struggles. Healthcare, inequality, education, and despair all stemmed from a distorted system engineered to extract value rather than empower people. Suddenly, dots connected. Society's issues weren't isolated; they were symptoms of corrupted money. Manipulated currency is a global epidemic, quietly draining value and eroding opportunity from everyone, everywhere. I saw its impact firsthand, both in the poverty of my hometown and in every corner of the world I traveled. Because no matter the currency, humans inevitably find ways to seize control of the money printer, and once they do, temptation always wins.

Was Bitcoin the solution? It seemed logical, yet almost too hopeful. Could it truly offer a way out? Why didn't many people see this? Maybe I was wrong. I dove in deeper, immersing myself in the Bitcoin community. The intellect I found was staggering; yet, more striking was their optimism. It stood in stark contrast to the quiet nihilism I'd known my entire life.

Bitcoin was different. It was a system built on rules, not rulers: pure mathematics, free from human error and corruption. It offered something unprecedented: *verifiable integrity*. You could see the code. You could verify the exact supply: 21 million, forever. No central banker could change it. No politician could inflate it away. Meanwhile, over 80% of the U.S. dollar supply has been printed since 2020, and by 2025, the printing has gone parabolic. This endless money printing is exactly how the current system was designed, reactively patching holes in a fundamentally broken structure. Bitcoin flips this model completely, creating a stable foundation of integrity and accountability upon which everything else can be built.

Bitcoin represented a blueprint for how money should have worked all along.

I discovered the power of lowering my time preference: if I worked diligently, saved intentionally, and converted my earnings into Bitcoin, freedom was attainable. I could step off the hamster wheel, breathe, and envision a future on my own terms. I was born into a world of walls: poverty, poor health, and broken money. Bitcoin showed me there was a way out.

Bitcoin made me question the systems around us. What else was fundamentally broken? The one that hit me hardest was our healthcare system.

In early 2024, I was suffering from chronic back pain caused by ice skating and was shuffled from specialist to specialist, physical therapist, and beyond. No one could help me. I spent nearly a year stuck in the system: waiting on appointments, chasing referrals, and endlessly repeating my story. Every time I visited my doctor, I'd ask questions, trying to understand my test results or treatment options. Instead of explaining, she'd turn around to her computer, type my symptoms into WebMD, and read verbatim whatever popped up, even printing it out for me. I remember sitting there, stunned. This was healthcare? A medical professional outsourcing her diagnosis to the same website I'd already checked at home?

I've heard this same story hundreds of times.

Every encounter reinforced that our healthcare system was reactive, not proactive. No one asked about my lifestyle. Nutrition was never discussed. Instead, I was offered prescriptions, steroid shots, and more drugs, all treatments designed to manage symptoms rather than resolve the root cause.

I decided to take matters into my own hands and heal myself, diving deep into the health and longevity rabbit hole. I soon realized that many chronic issues could be improved or completely reversed with just three things: diet, sleep, and exercise. No pills. No prescriptions. Just foundations.

The more I learned, the more obvious it became that I could no longer outsource my well-being, just as Bitcoin had taught me not to outsource control of my money. Taking self-custody had empowered me financially. Health was no different. That was the turning point. I had to become the custodian of my own body, just as I'd become the custodian of my own wealth.

So why wasn't this knowledge promoted? Why was simple, empowering information so hard to find? Why wasn't any of this taught in school? It was another system, like finance, designed to keep people dependent instead of empowered. A healthy, informed population isn't profitable.

The same strategy appears in both finance and healthcare: keep complexity alive and make everything feel too confusing to question. It made me wonder how many things we've accepted, not because they make sense, but because they've always been there. Things so deeply woven into our upbringing that we stopped even noticing them, let alone questioning them. Almost like a religion.

It's especially strange now, in the so-called Information Age. We have access to more knowledge than any generation before us; yet, most people are still trapped in outdated ideas about money, health, and how the world works. Maybe that's because we grew up before the internet changed everything, when information was scarce and systems felt untouchable. Back then, you accepted what you were told because it was the only version of the story you had. And even now, with everything at our fingertips, that old programming still runs deep.

Why are we so conditioned to trust these systems? How did they get put in place? Why do they dictate so much of our lives, yet so few understand how they work?

These systems were built to react once the damage is done. Reactive systems don't mitigate risk; they manage fallout. The **Federal Reserve** (The Fed) responds after markets crash. Doctors intervene once you're already sick. We've accepted reaction as normal.

Maybe it's time we asked why.

Who benefits from a world where we're always catching up, financially, physically, mentally, yet never truly ahead? What if these systems weren't designed to serve us, but to contain us? What if the only way out isn't to escape them, but to build something better in parallel?

That shift in perspective led me down a new path. If the systems weren't designed to save me, maybe the right tools, mindset, and protocols could. What began as survival became something else entirely. A search for resilience. For truth. For sovereignty.

That's where this story really begins.

Chapter 2

Proof of Work: Effort, Energy, and Earning What Matters

Don't give yourself the option to fail.

That was the line I kept repeating in 2014 as I packed up my desk. It was the year I walked away from corporate life to start my own film production company.

I hated office life. Long hours. Endless meetings. A boss who controlled my time. It gave me just enough money to survive, just enough comfort to stay quiet, but never enough freedom to build something better. The job consumed my life, leaving no room for what I actually wanted. It was just another system I needed to escape.

I looked around at my coworkers, hunched in identical cubicles beneath fluorescent lights, doing the same thing every day. The windowless office blurred mind-numbing days into nights; sometimes I went entire shifts without seeing daylight.

This made me ask... *Why?*

Did you make the world better? Did you use your time for something that mattered? Did you love your job? Did you wake up excited and eager to go in?

I didn't meet anyone who said yes.

There was always a quiet fear in the air: without a steady paycheck, you'd never make it. That stepping out on your own meant inevitable failure.

On my first day, HR told me it was "by far the best place to work." *Based on what?* I thought. You've never left. You've never seen anything else. You haven't tested the system. You've just stayed safely inside it.

When I announced I was leaving to start my own thing, I was told I was "jumping off a cliff." But I had tested the system. My whole life had been a series of experiments, proving I could survive *and* thrive outside the line.

Leaving wasn't quitting. It was reclaiming something that had always been mine: freedom. Stepping out of comfort wasn't reckless; staying inside it was suffocating.

In college, I chose video production as my major. Not one adult in my life supported that decision. Not one. Everyone pushed me toward something practical, like accounting. Something safe. But I didn't want safety; I wanted sovereignty. I wanted to study something I genuinely loved and was passionate about. I'd known this was my path since I was 15, spending nearly every free moment shooting and editing. To me, filmmaking wasn't just a hobby. It was my way out, my ticket to a different life.

While other students drifted through classes, checking boxes to graduate, I treated college like my one chance to build a career and escape my previous life. I was always filming something: TV shows, short films, freelance gigs, seizing any opportunity to sharpen my craft. I worked late nights editing footage on slow, outdated computers in dimly lit rooms and spent early mornings hauling gear to sets.

I worked two, sometimes three jobs at a time, doing whatever it took to keep moving forward. I was a resident assistant in the dorms, waited tables, served food in the dining hall, and took catering jobs on weekends. I also landed an editing role with the university's athletic department and produced community programs at the local public access TV station, writing, shooting, editing, and working continuously to build my skills. I didn't wait for opportunities. I made them.

Guyana

I spent countless late nights editing a video series for one of my professors. As a thank you, he invited me on a trip that would change my life.

A few months later, I boarded a plane to Guyana. It was the summer after my sophomore year, and at just twenty years old, I traveled alongside my documentary professor to teach a filmmaking course at the University of Guyana. My role was to introduce students, completely new to documentary storytelling, to the basics of editing. The university provided us with only a small trailer, a handful of aging desktops, and a couple of outdated cameras. It was bare-bones, but enough to make it work. By the end of the summer, our students had created Guyana's first-ever documentary TV series, built entirely from their own projects.

Nothing worked in Guyana. Electricity cut out regularly. Tap water wasn't drinkable. Bureaucracy crawled forward at an excruciating pace. Cockroaches bigger than your hand scurried openly across floors and walls. A nationwide trash strike had left months of garbage piled in the streets, fermenting under the tropical sun. Despite all of this, our students showed up every single day, eager to learn and patient with every setback.

One evening, I poured a beer and placed it next to a glass of water from the faucet. The beer was a lighter shade of brown. That was the water we were supposed to drink…so we stuck to beer for safety.

Later that summer, on our way to film interviews in a village near the Guyana–Brazil border, we got stranded deep in the Amazon. The locals called it the cocaine highway, one of the most dangerous corridors in South America. We were baking under 120-degree heat with only a tarp, a machete, and a single case of water for eleven people. Monkeys swung in the trees above us, fire ants attacked my legs, streams of blood mixing with sweat, while we waited, helpless. No phone. No service. No map. No food. No one knew where we were.

The only thing I let myself think was *I'm not going to die here.*

Hours melted into days. Nights were pitch-black, alive with unsettling noises from the jungle around us. Our driver, wearing a giant cross around his neck, openly took hits of cocaine right in front of us, eyes glazed and unfocused. Between futile attempts to fix our broken-down van, he'd obsessively pick through his toolbox, lifting tools one by one, staring blankly, clearly having no idea what to do.

We were deep into the journey, too far to walk back in that oppressive heat. We carefully divided the last few packs of cheese and crackers, rationed our dwindling water, and hoped for the best.

Finally, a van approached from the opposite direction. Relief flooded us; maybe we could finally escape the jungle. Our driver approached, exchanged a few hurried words, and then, to our disbelief, jumped into their vehicle. Without a single word to us, they sped off into the distance. Had he gone to find help? We had no idea. We stared at each other, confusion and anxiety mixing in the unbearable heat. We filmed everything using dated mini DV tape cameras with notoriously short battery lives, capturing each uncertain moment until, one by one, our batteries died.

At the start of day three, by some miracle, our driver returned with a mechanic and managed to fix our van. But the worst wasn't over. What should have been an eight-hour trip became a five-day ordeal. After escaping the jungle, we hit the savannahs, flooded and thick with waist-high mud. Nearly fifty times we piled out, shoulder-to-shoulder, pushing and slipping through the thick sludge. It was grueling, chaotic, and dangerous, but each step taught me something crucial: control is fragile, and when forced to adapt, you discover exactly how little you need to survive.

By the time we finally reached the village, we were starving. Someone brought us a platter of meat, origin unknown. I didn't ask. At that point, we were just grateful to eat.

When I finally returned to the U.S., everything looked different. Just turning on the tap felt like a luxury. I saw clearly how much we take for granted, how much just works without us even noticing. These photos show it better than words can (Figure 1). I was twenty, inexperienced, and thrown into chaos, but earning that perspective was its own kind of **proof of work**: an idea central to Bitcoin that means valuable outcomes require real effort, energy, and sacrifice. It permanently changed the way I see everything.

Figure 1: Van stranded in Guyana 2010. Photos by Erin E. Malone.

India

After Guyana, I applied for an internship with the Miss Universe Organization. I figured it might be slightly more glamorous. (Spoiler: it wasn't.) The following year, I traveled through India, Mexico, the Dominican Republic, Guatemala, and Panama, doing charity work and media coverage.

The locations changed, but the lessons deepened. That year forced me to grow. I learned how to appreciate what I had, but also how to push myself. I had to create a short film on the fly in every country we visited. Some trips involved hitting three countries in one week. I was filming 16 hours a day, editing on the plane, delivering final cuts with no time to waste. It was run-and-gun. Fast, raw, unpredictable. And it taught me things no classroom ever could, how to hone my craft under pressure, optimize every minute, and build resilience by embracing the chaos.

Resilience Is Proof of Work

Building resilience is proof of work. It's earned, not inherited. You don't become resilient by staying safe; you earn it by stepping into situations that force you to adapt. Discomfort is the cost of growth.

I was 21 years old and still relatively fresh out of my small rural town in Appalachia. Despite the eye-opening experience in Guyana, I felt completely unprepared when thrown into some of the most chaotic places on Earth. I had no phone, no itinerary, and a camera in hand. My job? Follow Miss Universe, document everything, and figure the rest out on the fly. I spent the next seven months traveling the world with a four-person crew: Miss Universe, myself, a creative director, and a single security guard.

India was my first stop after Guyana. And it made Guyana feel like the warm-up.

We traveled there for the Save the Girl Child campaign, addressing India's ongoing struggle with female infanticide and the dowry system. Just weeks before we arrived, thousands of baby girl fetuses had been discovered in a river. Tensions ran high, and our presence drew enormous crowds everywhere we went.

Each day brought a new city: no warnings, no maps, and no clear plans. We'd step out of the car and be swallowed immediately by thousands of people desperate for a glimpse of Miss Universe. I had lens caps ripped off my cameras; hands reached for my gear from all directions. Chaos became our new normal. I spent sixteen-hour days with her for seven months straight, filming every moment, the good, the difficult, and everything in between. Experiences like that either bond you for life or make you enemies. Thankfully, we became friends.

One afternoon, we joined a march with over 10,000 schoolchildren and parents (Figure 2). Miss Universe was brought onto a makeshift platform to give a speech. Standing beside her, camera rolling, I suddenly felt the entire crowd surge forward. In seconds, our small platform was engulfed.

Our single security guard grabbed Miss Universe and shoved through the mass of bodies, creating a narrow path. My job was clear: keep filming, no matter what. But halfway through the chaos, I lost sight of her. Realizing I had no idea where they were heading, I jumped into the rushing sea of people and immediately got trampled. Arms, legs, and bodies pressed in from every direction, knocking me to the ground. My heart pounded as I curled protectively around my cameras, shielding the equipment the best I could.

I forced myself to my feet, somehow unharmed, gear miraculously intact. Pushing through the crowd, adrenaline surging, I finally emerged, but Miss Universe and the other two members of our tiny team had vanished.

I stood there, alone. Twenty-one years old, lost in a remote Indian village. I was the only white person for miles, unable to speak the language, holding expensive camera gear, with absolutely no idea where to go next. No phone. No itinerary. I didn't even know the name of the place we were staying that night. But I knew one thing: I had to figure it out.

I started walking, asking anyone who looked approachable if they'd seen Miss Universe. Two men pointed confidently in opposite directions. Half an hour passed, and I felt that familiar uncertainty creeping in; this was Guyana all over again. But then I heard something rare: two little girls speaking English.

I asked if they knew anything about Miss Universe. Their faces lit up. "She's coming to our school today!" My instincts told me to follow them. Taking me by the hand, they led me through winding streets and up a hill to their school. When we arrived, a teacher confirmed that Miss Universe was, in fact, coming.

An hour later, a car finally pulled up. The window rolled down, and Miss Universe's eyes widened when she saw me. "Oh my god," she said. "I thought you might have died."

Before leaving, I had her sign autographs for the two little girls who may have saved my life.

One night in India, Miss Universe became violently ill, throwing up repeatedly. Our creative director was on the phone with the president of Miss Universe, who insisted I film it. Stunned, I asked, "You want me to film her…throwing up?" She confirmed, "Yes." I refused. She was furious. After all, that was my job, but it felt wrong. There was a line I wouldn't cross. It felt surreal to be 21 years old, standing up to the president of Miss Universe. I never imagined I'd have to do something like that. But that moment taught me to speak up, set boundaries, and prepared me for future uncomfortable conversations with bosses and clients. Capturing the story mattered, but trust mattered more. Without that trust, I'd never be able to capture the honest interviews and authentic moments my work required. Crossing that line wasn't storytelling. It was exploitation. Holding firm in moments like that took courage, clarity, and integrity.

India was relentless, a continuous stream of chaos. Day after day, it tested my patience, my stomach (I was sick nearly every day), and my instincts. It taught me to adapt, think fast, and deliver under intense circumstances. It was execution under pressure.

That was proof of work.

Figure 2: India January 2011. Photos by Erin E. Malone.

Guatemala came later during the Miss Universe internship. We were working with the organization Aid for AIDS in Guatemala City's red-light districts, distributing condoms and teaching sex workers about safe practices. I remember sitting with women who quietly told us they slept with ten, sometimes fifteen men a day, just to feed their kids. The reality was harsh, bleak, and almost impossible to comprehend.

I was filming Miss Universe as we walked through a narrow, dimly lit hallway lined with doors. Each room had nothing more than a dirty mattress tossed onto the floor and a bucket of water; there was no running water, no sanitation. Suddenly, shouting erupted. Angry voices echoed down the cramped hallway, too fast for me to understand. Men ran toward us, and before I could fully grasp what was happening, I caught a glimpse of a man pulling a gun.

Our security guard reacted instantly, stepping in front of us and confronting the man, his voice firm but calm. In seconds, he had diffused the situation, then grabbed Miss Universe and me and shoved us quickly into a waiting car. "Go straight to the hotel," he told the driver. "Lock the doors. Do not stop for anyone."

As we sped through the chaotic city streets, I kept filming, hands steady, adrenaline sharp but controlled. Another day, another close call. That was the job: capture the story, no matter how dangerous or chaotic it got.

I'm not saying you should throw yourself into danger. I wouldn't recommend it.

But stepping outside your comfort zone, really stepping out, does something to you.

It sharpens your instincts.

It stretches your perspective.

It makes you resourceful in ways you never knew you had.

When things fall apart, many people become paralyzed by fear, unable to think clearly or move forward. But when you've trained yourself to handle uncertainty, you don't freeze, you act.

That same mindset kept me going in Guyana. It's the same mindset I leaned into when I walked away from corporate life and started my business. Resilience is a skill, one earned through effort, repetition, and real discomfort.

Even after I built something of my own, a successful production business, life kept testing me. Wildfires hit. Jobs vanished overnight. Then came

COVID. Budgets dried up, contracts disappeared, and it felt like watching my life collapse in slow motion. Year after year, I had to rebuild, constantly forced to adapt.

But I didn't quit. I learned to work smarter, trim the fat, focus on the signal, not the noise, prioritize relationships that mattered, and work on projects that paid off long-term. I learned to grind and adapt strategically.

Because freedom doesn't come from coasting. It comes from putting in the kind of effort that compounds over time. Effort that stacks, that builds momentum, that keeps you standing when everything around you shakes.

Was it easy? Hell no.

Was it worth it? Absolutely.

I worked. I hustled. I learned discipline. I never gave myself the option to fail. Over time, I became my own boss... my own *system*.

Let's call it... *proof of work*.

Leaving the comfort of a steady paycheck was like seeing the Matrix clearly for the first time. The thing I believed was essential, the security I thought I needed, was the very thing holding me back. Walking away seemed reckless to everyone around me, but for me it was an act of reclamation.

Everything that mattered: escaping poverty, gaining freedom, healing my body, and reclaiming my time, required genuine effort. Real work. Proof of work wasn't just a Bitcoin principle. It defined my life long before I had words for it. All those lessons, the hustle, the grind, the relentless adaptation, finally had a name.

I built my life on proof of work. The same principle secures the hardest money on Earth.

Bitcoin Mining Is Proof of Work

So what exactly is "Proof of Work," and why does it matter?

The foundational idea was first proposed by Cynthia Dwork and Moni Naor in 1993, who suggested using computational power to fight email spam and denial-of-service attacks. By requiring senders to perform a small amount of work, they made it expensive to send mass messages. In 1997, Adam Back expanded on this idea with Hashcash, a system designed specifically to combat email spam. In 2009, **Satoshi Nakamoto** adapted and popularized Proof of Work as a central innovation in Bitcoin, using it to secure the network, prevent fraud, and fairly reward miners. Now that you understand Proof of Work's origins, here's how Bitcoin miners put it into practice.

Bitcoin miners, specialized computers called **ASICs**, secure the network by repeatedly guessing random, extremely large numbers. This computational process is known as **hashing**.

Every miner competes to find a number that matches the network's difficulty target, which automatically adjusts every 2,016 blocks (approximately every two weeks) to ensure new blocks are created roughly every 10 minutes. This **difficulty adjustment** acts as Bitcoin's built-in feedback mechanism, maintaining fairness, stability, and predictability no matter how many miners join or leave the network.

When a miner guesses correctly, they earn the right to add the next block of transactions to the blockchain. As a reward, they're paid in bitcoin: the **block subsidy** plus transaction fees. Approximately every four years (or every 210,000 blocks), this block subsidy is cut in half, an event known as "**the halving**." The halving gradually reduces the issuance of new bitcoin, ensuring scarcity. This process continues until around the year 2140, when the final fraction of bitcoin will be mined, ultimately capping Bitcoin's total supply at 21 million coins.

The more miners actively mining on the network, the more computational effort is required, making Bitcoin increasingly secure and resistant to attacks. Anyone attempting to alter the blockchain would need to redo the proof of work for every previous block, an almost impossible task requiring enormous amounts of energy, time, and hardware.

It's not magic. It's code. It's math. It's computing power + time + energy. Miners are rewarded for what they've proven: *that they've done the work*.

But even running a miner requires proof of work. It's not plug-and-play. It's a brutally competitive industry where profitability isn't guaranteed. To succeed, you need cheap electricity, efficient hardware, a smart strategy, and constant adaptability. Just like in life, simply showing up isn't enough. You must find your edge, outwork the competition, and optimize every step.

People love to say success comes from luck. They're wrong. Success has nothing to do with luck. It's grueling, messy, and relentless. It doesn't matter if you're mining Bitcoin or chasing another goal in life, the process is the same. Most people never see beneath the surface. They miss the hours spent troubleshooting, problem-solving, and planning. All they see is the finished product.

Proof of work can lead to unexpected opportunities. Around the world, individuals and companies running Bitcoin mining operations constantly discover creative ways to transform waste or inefficiency into valuable resources. A remarkable example is heat, a mining byproduct once completely dismissed. Today, miners repurpose this heat into real, tangible value.

I heat my home using a Bitcoin miner. I even heat my hot tub with one. I call it the Hot Tub Mine Machine. Miners everywhere have started repurposing excess heat for drying clothes, curing wood, even distilling maple syrup and whiskey.

If you're already heating your home with electricity, you can swap out your space heater for an ASIC that costs about $200 *and* get paid in bitcoin while keeping warm. It's this kind of creative, outside-the-box thinking that drives real breakthroughs.

Miners operate on the edge. They constantly push efficiency, squeezing value from every watt of energy. In 2010, Bitcoin's creator, Satoshi Nakamoto, said, "Bitcoin generation should end up where it's cheapest. Maybe that will be in cold climates where there's electric heat, where it would be essentially free. "

Today, miners in cold climates across the globe are proving him right: turning heat into value, effort into security, and wasted energy into opportunity.

Proof of Work at Scale

When it comes to Bitcoin, Proof of Work extends far beyond verifying transactions. It's driving real-world innovation across energy, infrastructure, and resilience.

In Texas, miners work alongside utility operators as flexible grid balancers, instantly powering down during peak electricity demand and quickly firing back up when energy is abundant. With massive wind and solar installations, Texas needs flexible consumers who can reliably soak up surplus energy. Bitcoin miners fill this role perfectly, stabilizing the grid, reducing waste, and making renewable energy projects economically viable.

But it goes deeper. Miners also incentivize the *overbuilding* of power generation beyond typical demand needs. Why? Because they act as a **buyer of last resort**, willing to consume excess electricity that would otherwise go unused. This dynamic encourages utilities to expand capacity, strengthen infrastructure, and prepare for volatility. The result: fewer blackouts, greater energy flexibility, and a more secure grid, especially during extreme weather events.

In August 2023, Bitcoin mining company Riot Platforms reported that they shut off 95% of their miners during Texas's harshest summer heatwaves. That move helped prevent rolling blackouts by easing pressure on the grid when demand spiked. Miners like Riot are even compensated through demand response agreements, getting paid not to use electricity during peak strain. These arrangements allow miners to stay profitable even when powered down, while helping utilities better plan and manage their operations. It's a win-win built on flexibility, economic incentives, and proof of work.

Across parts of Africa, Bitcoin miners directly fund infrastructure by building out electricity grids, internet access, roads, and creating local jobs in areas that previously had none. In 2021, 43% of Africans, around 600 million people, lacked access to electricity. The reasons are complex: underfunded governments, geographic barriers, and systemic corruption. Traditional infrastructure development often stalls in these regions. Bitcoin mining offers a new model.

Enter Gridless, a company tapping into remote hydro, geothermal, and biomass energy sources to power local Bitcoin mines in Africa. These renewable sources are often stranded, but abundant, yet too remote to monetize. Gridless channels this energy into **microgrids**: small-scale, decentralized power systems that operate independently from national grids. These microgrids deliver electricity to villages previously without power, creating employment opportunities, boosting local economies, and empowering communities.

Mining again acts as the buyer of last resort, creating a stable revenue stream that justifies the cost of building and maintaining these grids. The energy that powers the miners also powers homes, schools, clinics, and small businesses. The Bitcoin earned helps fund the expansion and upkeep of these systems. The result is affordable electricity, jobs, economic growth, and improved infrastructure in places the global development system has long ignored.

In Finland, Bitcoin mining is being reimagined as part of the country's essential heating infrastructure. With long winters and heavy demand for thermal energy, companies are turning mining's so-called waste heat into a valuable asset. Hashlabs Mining is piloting hydro-cooled ASIC miners that heat water to 70°C. This heated water is fed into district heating systems, warming nearby greenhouses, industrial facilities, and public buildings. Rather than allowing thermal byproducts to dissipate, they are captured, circulated, and put to work, displacing fossil fuels and enhancing local energy efficiency.

Meanwhile, Marathon Digital Holdings has scaled its own district heating initiative in Finland. What began in June 2024 as a pilot project heating 11,000 homes in the Satakunta region has since expanded to serve approximately 80,000 residents. Using centralized systems that distribute hot water through underground pipelines, Marathon repurposes the heat from Bitcoin mining to warm entire communities. This shift turns miners into dual-purpose infrastructure, providing both financial and thermal energy. The approach can reduce energy costs, ease grid congestion, and accelerate the adoption of renewable energy by making better use of local generation.

What looks like waste is often just unused potential. Once you adopt proof of work as a mindset, you stop seeing inefficiency and start seeing opportunity. **Stranded energy** becomes useful. Overlooked regions become investable. What others discard, you put to work. From Texas to Kenya to Finland, Bitcoin mining is quietly rewiring how we think about energy, infrastructure, and value.

At its core, proof of work is a response to entropy. Left unchecked, everything drifts toward disorder: money devalues, systems break down, and resilience fades. Fighting that drift requires sustained energy, adaptive design, and continuous work. Miners do this every day. They stabilize fragile grids, recycle waste heat, and monetize overlooked energy sources. Instead of surrendering to decay, they transform it into tangible value.

We'll further explore entropy's role in Bitcoin and longevity in Chapter 8.

Proof of Work in the Body

Just like Bitcoin, your body is an energy-based system. It responds to stress, adapts to pressure, and becomes stronger through consistent effort.

You can't fake strength. You can't buy endurance. No one else can do the work for you.

Muscle mass, metabolic health, and quality sleep, all of these things must be earned.

Your body is proof of work.

Every training session, every fasting window, every morning you move instead of hitting snooze. That's your hash rate. That's your input. That's you saying, I showed up again. Your body thrives on consistency and effort. Proof of work in the body is also your response to entropy. Without intentional effort, your health naturally drifts toward disorder: muscle mass declines, metabolism slows, and energy fades. Every deliberate action you take today fights back against this natural pull toward decay. Like Bitcoin, the more consistent work you put in, the more resilient the system becomes.

Doing the work matters, but tracking it matters too. Proof of work means paying close attention to your inputs and outcomes. Maybe that's recording sleep quality and testing meal timing, supplements, or room temperature. Maybe it's stepping onto a scale each week, checking bloodwork every few months, or logging progress in the gym. Whatever you're focused on, measuring helps separate genuine progress from guesswork. It clarifies what truly works for your body, your goals, and your life.

Proof of work demands two resources you can't fake: time and energy. Those investments carry weight, whether you're mining Bitcoin, optimizing your health, or forging a life on your own terms.

Want to start? Get a tracker.

Apple Watch, Oura Ring, Whoop, Fitbit. Get whatever resonates with you.

Measure your baseline.
Experiment thoughtfully.
Monitor the outcomes.
Adjust based on results.

Repeat. That's how real progress happens.

Not sure what to track? Whether it's body weight, muscle mass, or blood work, the same principle applies: test, adjust, repeat. Throughout this book, we'll touch on metrics like VO_2 max, heart rate recovery, and **biological age** testing. In Chapter 6, we'll focus more specifically on key indicators like heart rate, heart rate variability, and sleep quality. The path is personal, but data gives you the clarity to move forward with confidence.

Learning as Proof of Work

Proof of work extends beyond your body or wallet; it shapes how you learn.

Information is everywhere. Distraction is too. With AI accelerating the pace of change, it's never been easier to get overwhelmed or misled. The ability to learn, unlearn, and relearn is no longer optional; it's survival. You don't give yourself the option to fail. You grind. You adapt. You build.

To thrive, you must continually update your mental frameworks, rewiring your brain as new technologies and insights emerge. Clinging to outdated beliefs or habits means falling behind. Adaptability is your greatest advantage. The future belongs to those who can rapidly recognize new realities, let go of what's no longer useful, and pivot decisively.

In health, new research, tools, and protocols constantly emerge. In Bitcoin, learning never stops. Monetary theory, energy, geopolitics, privacy, and sovereignty are rabbit holes with no bottom.

That's why learning itself is proof of work.

It's slow, layered, and compounds steadily over time. It sharpens your ability to see clearly, tune into the signal, and cut through the noise. Done right, it means actively seeking out smarter people who challenge your thinking, sharpen your understanding, and push you to grow. It requires humility to remain teachable and discipline to keep showing up.

But not all success is earned through proof of work. In our current economic system, genuine learning and growth are often undervalued. Nearly half of publicly traded U.S. companies are unprofitable, kept alive not by innovation, but by cheap debt, easy money, and speculation. These "zombie corporations" survive precisely because the system doesn't require true learning, adaptation, or real value creation. Instead, artificially low interest rates and endless money printing delay necessary consequences and reward complacency. It's an inflation-fueled illusion. (We'll explore this further in Chapter 4.)

True resilience and lasting success demand authentic proof of work: continuous learning, consistent effort, and meaningful value creation.

Your future isn't free, it's earned… every day, with every decision and every block you add. That's proof of work.

Mining Reward: Open-Source Learning

The internet has streamlined knowledge. Everything you want to learn is now at your fingertips. No gatekeepers, no limits. Pick a skill, dive in, and mine your own education. The world is open-source, take advantage.

Bitcoin Recipe: Run Your Own Node

In Bitcoin, the chain grows block by block. Life works exactly the same way. Your health, wealth, and mind are all built one block at a time. And just like Bitcoin, each block strengthens the entire chain, growing more resilient with consistency and effort.

Ready to take your first digital proof-of-work step?

Ingredients:

- Raspberry Pi 4 (or higher) or an old laptop

- 2TB SSD (Solid State Drive)

- Ethernet cable

- Power supply

- Case for Raspberry Pi (optional but recommended)

- Umbrel or MyNode OS

Instructions:

1. Connect your Raspberry Pi or laptop to the SSD.

2. Plug your device directly into your router using the Ethernet cable.

3. Connect to power and switch on.

4. Install Umbrel or MyNode OS by following the respective setup guides online.

5. Sync the blockchain (this initial sync can take a few days).

6. Start verifying your own Bitcoin transactions, no middlemen or banks required.

Advanced users: Install and run Bitcoin Core directly on your old laptop.

Congratulations: You've just reclaimed your financial sovereignty.

Proof of Work Recovery Smoothie Recipe

You've worked. You've trained. Now it is time to recover without wrecking your metabolic progress.

Ingredients:

- 1 cup unsweetened almond or oat milk

- ½ frozen banana

- ½ cup wild blueberries

- 1 tbsp ground flaxseed

- ½ tsp turmeric

- 1-inch fresh ginger (or ¼ tsp powdered ginger)

- 1 scoop plant-based protein

- Dash of cinnamon

- Optional: pinch of black pepper (to enhance turmeric absorption)

- Optional: 3–5 grams creatine monohydrate *(supports muscle recovery, strength, and cognitive performance)*

Instructions:

1. Combine all ingredients in a blender.

2. Blend until smooth and creamy.

3. Pour into a glass and enjoy immediately.

Blend it, recover, and show up again tomorrow. Proof of work earns the reward. This is yours.

Chapter 3

Low Time Preference: Delaying Gratification for Future Freedom

I discovered Bitcoin in 2017 on Facebook. A post caught my eye: "Wish I'd waited to buy Bitcoin." Curious, I googled it. Futuristic. Intriguing. I bought a little to see what happened.

Within three weeks, my modest investment tripled. I'd never seen money behave that way before. For a brief moment, excitement took over. I imagined all the ways I could immediately spend or reinvest this unexpected windfall. Logic told me to cash out, take the quick win, and celebrate. The temptation was strong, but something deeper held me back.

I paused and thought about what money really meant to me. Growing up in Appalachia, I knew exactly how much sweat and time went into earning even a few dollars. I'd been babysitting and tutoring other people's kids since I was nine years old. At eleven, I was responsible for a nine-year-old boy who once tried setting off fireworks inside the house. He was practically my size, and I vividly remember tackling him to the ground and wrestling away the fireworks. Some days I'd watch him for ten hours straight, and afterward I'd carefully set aside the $20 bill I earned, stacking each one in a safe place for the future. Every saved bill felt like another step toward something bigger, something I couldn't yet fully see. I knew the waiting would be worth it.

As a teenager, I worked at a local restaurant making $3 an hour. Smoking bans had just been implemented, yet my boss instructed me to put out ashtrays for customers, quickly hiding them if a certain car pulled into the parking lot, likely a health inspector. Everything in that place was deep-fried, and no matter how many showers I took or how often I washed my clothes, I always reeked of grease and cigarettes. Old men slid quarters across their tables with crude remarks, expecting coffee refills and a smile.

I did this in addition to working shifts at the local grocery store. One summer, I even took a job as a janitor's assistant at a school, scrubbing toilets, painting fences, and waxing floors. I did whatever needed to be done. Every single dollar I earned was a battle, a genuine struggle of time, energy, and dignity.

So when I finally saved enough money after years of babysitting, tutoring, waitressing, cashiering, and cleaning toilets to buy my first camera, it wasn't just about owning a camera. That camera represented everything I'd endured, every sacrifice, every delayed gratification. That purchase changed my life, setting me on the path to filmmaking, traveling, and eventually discovering Bitcoin.

Given all that, seeing my small investment triple effortlessly in a few weeks felt surreal. It didn't feel earned; it felt insane. Then, almost immediately, Bitcoin crashed. My gains evaporated just as fast. Headlines screamed about Ponzi schemes and bubbles bursting. The crypto space, filled with scams and hype-driven altcoins, felt chaotic and unreliable. Logic again told me to sell and salvage whatever scraps remained, but that quiet voice, born from years of patience, disciplined saving, and the life-changing reward of that first camera, insisted there was something bigger here. While I didn't fully understand money yet, my initial research had given me enough confidence in Bitcoin's potential to hold on, echoing the patience I'd learned as a kid.

I refused to lock in losses and even bought a bit more as prices kept dropping. My understanding stayed surface-level for a long time. The deeper story, the bigger "why" behind Bitcoin, still hadn't clicked.

It wasn't until 2020 that the pieces finally fell into place. Locked inside during the pandemic, I went deep down the Bitcoin rabbit hole. I consumed everything: podcasts, books, articles, and hours spent listening to people smarter than me on Clubhouse (an audio-based social app). I finally understood what money really was: how our financial system is fundamentally broken, how fiat currencies inevitably lose value, and how Bitcoin was the solution.

The word "**fiat**" means "by authoritative decree." Every paper currency you've ever touched, dollars, pesos, euros, yen, lira, yuan, or any of the 180 government-issued currencies today, has been created by governments or central banks, backed only by trust in their authority. These currencies aren't backed by gold or tangible assets, and their value inevitably erodes over time as more money is printed.

The U.S. dollar was once loosely tied to gold, but that backing was always fragile. Citizens had their gold confiscated in 1933, and by 1971, the U.S. abandoned the gold standard entirely. Since then, the dollar has been "backed" by nothing, just political promises and the illusion of control. No scarcity. No accountability. Just an endless supply created at the push of a button.

We'll dive deeper into exactly why and how our current financial system is broken in Chapter 4.

At that moment, everything shifted. My casual interest turned into full conviction. My earlier instincts to hold were validated, now backed by understanding. I went from casually holding to full-on HODL mode (see HODL mining reward). Consumption took a back seat; saving became my priority. I tried to own almost nothing, intentionally living cheaply and funneling every spare penny into Bitcoin.

Those choices felt tough at first, but soon became second nature. Low time preference, the heart of this chapter, means prioritizing the long-term over immediate gratification. It evolved from financial jargon into the foundation of my daily life. Every stacked **satoshi** (small units of bitcoin) felt like a vote for the future I believed in, reshaping my approach not only to money but also to health, sleep, exercise, and nutrition.

HODLing taught patience and clarity. It was an exercise in financial discipline, showing that real value comes from remaining calm amid chaos, zooming out, and steadily building for years instead of chasing quick wins.

The lesson was clear: the future belongs to those willing to wait.

The patience and discipline I learned from HODLing Bitcoin quickly spilled over into every part of my life: health, habits, even sleep.

Mining Reward: HODL

The year was 2013. Bitcoin was crashing, again. A user on the Bitcoin Talk forum while drunk and frustrated, meant to type "I AM HOLDING." Instead, he wrote: "I AM HODLING." The typo stuck.

HODL became a rallying cry, a mindset. A signal that you've done the work, you know what you hold, and you're not selling just because the market panicked. You're here for the long game.

Beyond Bitcoin: Low Time Preference as a Lifestyle

HODLing Bitcoin reshaped my entire approach to life. I spent years chasing quick wins, fast money, instant comforts, and easy conveniences, but quick hits don't last. Bitcoin forced me to slow down. It taught me that real value demands consistency and discipline. It didn't just change how I viewed money; it changed how I perceived time itself.

This low time preference mindset quickly spilled into everyday decisions. Now, whenever I'm tempted to snack impulsively, scroll mindlessly, or skip a workout, I pause. I ask myself, *"Am I hungry... or just bored?"* This simple check-in creates space for better choices.

I vividly remember a moment from earlier this year. I've never been a runner. In fact, I've always avoided it. But I'd decided to start running short distances, just a mile or two, trying to push my VO_2 max (maximum oxygen uptake during intense exercise) and break my personal heart-rate records. On my first few runs, I barely made it a quarter-mile without stopping. It felt impossible. But something clicked: this was exactly like the early days with Bitcoin. Gains didn't happen overnight; it was about consistently showing up, regardless of immediate results. Soon, running became less of a chore and more of a game. I'd log a new high score on my Apple Watch, beat yesterday's record, and repeat.

I rock climb, skate, and lift weights regularly, but running provided a different sort of feedback, something immediate, measurable, and addictive.

Clear data made progress visible, just like stacking sats and watching my savings grow.

The results of those disciplined runs were slow but transformative. My body fat percentage dropped significantly, my recovery improved, and my energy levels stabilized. None of these improvements came from shortcuts or quick hacks. They came from consistently showing up, putting in the reps, prioritizing sleep, cooking nutritious meals, and consciously trading immediate comfort for long-term strength and vitality.

Adopting a low time preference became a lifestyle. It shaped how I trained, ate, slept, saved, and made purchasing decisions. It meant playing the long game, even when nobody was watching, even when immediate rewards weren't apparent.

Just like Bitcoin, our time is inherently scarce. Bitcoin's supply is permanently capped at 21 million coins. Similarly, the time we have in life is limited. But here's the paradox: deliberately delaying gratification and consistently investing in your health actually give you more time. It increases your lifespan, your healthspan, and your ability to show up fully for the people and projects you deeply care about. Every early bedtime, every intermittent fast, every tough workout compounds over years. Each intentional decision helps you reclaim time that might otherwise be lost to fatigue, inflammation, or illness. You're actively slowing your body's natural breakdown, creating order from chaos.

Today, I regularly ask myself: *Will future Erin appreciate this decision? Will ten-minutes-from-now Erin thank me? What about fifty-years-from-now Erin?* Occasionally, I even pause to give past Erin a high-five through the space-time continuum, grateful for all the small decisions she made along the way. I think back and feel genuine appreciation for younger Erin, who resisted impulse spending, skipped dessert, or went for that uncomfortable run when it was the last thing she felt like doing.

Viewing life through that lens changes everything. It doesn't mean eliminating spontaneity or enjoyment. Some moments are worth the tradeoff, like being able to say I once smoked weed with Miss USA. Not every decision has to optimize lifespan. But my baseline choices now have intention. They're structured around building vitality and freedom rather than eroding them.

We live in a world designed for convenience and instant gratification. Choosing to pause, even briefly, and act intentionally is rare. But those rare, intentional choices compound into life-changing results. It's not flashy. It's not always fun. But it works.

People spend decades building careers, yet most won't invest even a single year developing habits to ensure they'll actually enjoy retirement in good health. This reality struck me deeply. Coming from a family and community where health often deteriorated prematurely, I knew firsthand the cost of neglecting long-term health choices.

Low time preference means valuing your future enough to take action today.

Let this sink in: in the U.S., the average **healthspan**, the years you live without major health issues, is approximately 63, while overall lifespan averages around 78.4 years. That's nearly two decades spent in decline, chronic pain, and missed opportunities. But this doesn't have to be your story.

By embracing low time preference and prioritizing consistent habits over immediate gratification, you can extend your healthspan, not just your lifespan.

Stack habits like you stack sats: slow, steady, and with your future self in mind.

Delayed Gratification in Both Systems

Bitcoin rewards those who delay gratification. So does your body.

With Bitcoin, you steadily stack sats, consistently adding small fractions rather than chasing speculative hype or quick gains. With health, you steadily stack disciplined habits like good nutrition, consistent exercise, and quality sleep, instead of relying on crash diets or quick-fix hacks. In both cases, you're choosing long-term stability over short-term thrills.

Delayed gratification isn't easy, but it's where the real leverage is. You train today to build strength and resilience, you'll need a decade from now. You stack sats today to secure freedom you'll deeply appreciate in the future. Whether strengthening your physical health or building your financial foundation, today's efforts protect your future self from becoming trapped, sick, or broke.

That's the essence of low time preference: putting in the effort now to honor your future self.

But it's more than just physical or financial effort; it's emotional effort, too. It's learning how to stay calm through discomfort, hold steady when things feel uncertain, and continuing to show up even when nobody else is watching or cheering you on.

It reminds me of holding Bitcoin through brutal bear markets, when everyone else panicked or mocked the idea. I wasn't guessing. I'd done the research and trusted my conviction. Similarly, making disciplined health choices often means ignoring the noise of quick-fix trends and trusting the fundamentals you've carefully built. You're not seeking immediate rewards; you're playing the long game.

Conviction like that isn't luck. It's earned through experience, consistent effort, and resilience. That's how low time preference truly works, and that's why delayed gratification isn't passive; it's one of the strongest decisions you can make for your future.

Patience Isn't Passive

Patience is dead. Our culture rewards speed, urgency, and instant results. We're wired to chase quick **dopamine** hits (the brain's reward chemical), betting on a trending memecoin, ordering DoorDash after a rough day, and endlessly refreshing social media for validation. Slowing down feels unnatural. Stillness feels like missing out.

I used to chase every quick win, scrolling, tapping, and reacting, caught up in a cycle of short-term rewards. But low time preference changed everything. It became clear to me that real growth often means deliberately choosing less so you can gain more: discipline over shortcuts, habits over hacks, and home-cooked meals instead of instant gratification.

Even small choices can shape better dopamine habits. For example, one reason I chose an Apple Watch without cellular reception was so I could deliberately leave my phone behind. My watch still tracks workouts and steps and lets me enjoy downloaded music or audiobooks, all without notifications, pings, or the temptation to scroll mindlessly. Removing distractions makes disciplined choices easier, allowing healthier dopamine loops to form naturally. *(Obviously, if you're exploring a new location, hiking alone, or anywhere you might need help, bring your phone! Safety first.)*

41

There are still moments when I'm tempted to skip a workout or reach for something unhealthy. Recently, I caught myself standing in front of the fridge, impulsively reaching for snacks. I wasn't hungry; I was restless, procrastinating, and seeking distraction. In that moment, I paused, took a deep breath, and consciously stepped away. *Have some water. Move your body. Change your scenery.* I reminded myself how indulgence would affect my metrics: my energy levels would dip, my sleep would suffer, my gains would stall or reverse. That simple mental shift, practiced regularly, rewires your brain to release dopamine after disciplined actions rather than before them.

Low time preference isn't about perfection. It's about recognizing that sometimes what we think we desperately want now is exactly what our future self hopes we'll avoid. It's choosing stillness over impulse, investment over indulgence.

Low time preference is the opposite of living like there's no tomorrow. It rejects nihilism. Instead, it says: *"I believe in the future, so I'll act accordingly. I'll eat for it. Train for it. Save for it. Build for it."*

Bitcoin drove this idea home for me. Instead of chasing temporary highs, I regularly ask myself: *"What decision today will my 80-year-old self thank me for?"* That's a question I never used to ask. However, Bitcoin shifted my perspective across years, decades, and even generations. Initially, it felt strange, maybe even dramatic, but soon it reshaped every daily choice. I started seeing each decision as a vote for the future I truly wanted: healthier, stronger, freer, and happier.

Low time preference is a commitment. It's intentionally shaping your priorities to invest in a life you'll genuinely enjoy for decades, not days. It's knowing that future freedom and long-term health are worth far more than a brief dopamine rush. It might mean asking yourself questions like: *"Do I really need that expensive new car, or is the one I have perfectly fine? Do I need this latest gadget, or can I comfortably live without it? Should I buy that sugary donut, or can I make a nutritious breakfast at home?"* For me, it means foregoing unnecessary purchases and investing the difference in Bitcoin. It means trading short-term sugar highs or impulsive comforts for long-term health and freedom. Yet low time preference doesn't mean sacrificing everything you enjoy. It simply means your baseline decisions are intentional and reflect the future you're building.

Ultimately, patience isn't passive. It's one of the most powerful choices you can make.

Mining Reward: Plant Something

One of my favorite low time preference activities is starting a garden. You don't get instant results. You dig, plant, water, and wait, sometimes for weeks, sometimes for months. But every small act compounds. Roots deepen. Growth happens quietly. One day, you walk outside, and there it is, real food made with your own effort.

Gardening rewires your brain. It teaches patience, presence, and trust in the process. It reminds you that not everything should be rushed. Some things are only valuable because they take time.

Blue Zones: Low Time Preference Lessons from Sardinia

Blue Zones are regions around the world known for exceptionally high concentrations of centenarians: people who live healthily to age 100 or older. These areas include Sardinia (Italy), Okinawa (Japan), Nicoya (Costa Rica), Icaria (Greece), and Loma Linda (California). Despite diverse geographies and cultures, these regions share common lifestyle habits that contribute to extraordinary longevity, such as plant-based diets, strong community bonds, low stress, and consistent physical activity.

Sometimes longevity is about slowing down, not rushing, and simply taking the stairs. Residents in Sardinia's mountainous Blue Zone region seamlessly integrate constant movement into their daily routines, naturally supporting their remarkable longevity. Due to the steep, rugged terrain, many homes are multi-story structures built directly onto slopes, making stair use unavoidable. Residents spend their days actively navigating steep hills as they run errands, visit friends, or tend gardens.

In Sardinia, residents routinely average over 12,000 steps a day through these ordinary activities. Traditional occupations like goat and sheep herding further reinforce this active lifestyle; herders regularly navigate challenging terrain, walking nearly eight miles daily, much of it uphill.

By contrast, older adults in America often relocate to single-story homes or nursing facilities specifically to avoid stairs and minimize physical effort. This unintentionally eliminates valuable daily movement essential for maintaining strength, balance, and metabolic health. Even more significantly, many become isolated, losing the sense of purpose, community engagement, and daily challenges that naturally accompany active lifestyles. Maintaining regular physical activity and social connection helps keep you mentally sharp and supports a vibrant, purposeful life well into your later years.

Living with a low time preference means intentionally choosing movement, even when it feels inconvenient or physically demanding in the short term. Small, consistent decisions, regularly taking stairs, walking hills, and naturally incorporating movement into your routine, accumulate significantly over time, profoundly enhancing your health, mobility, and longevity.

Systems, Habits, and Dopamine Rewiring

We don't have to blindly follow existing systems; we can build our own. Daily routines, diet choices, workout plans, sleep habits, financial strategies: we create these systems ourselves. The goal isn't rigid perfection but creating a reliable foundation you can consistently trust.

Markets collapse. Headlines distort reality. Bitcoin, however, is designed to withstand the chaos of human error and failing systems. When your net worth drops 60% overnight or your fiat salary melts steadily away due to inflation, you can stay calm knowing you're backed by a system built for resilience.

Trusting these new systems didn't happen automatically. It took hours of reading, researching, measuring, and questioning what money actually is and how my body truly functions. I had to clearly identify what's broken in our financial system and what's missing from how we typically approach health, and then create better, more reliable systems. I put in the work, built understanding, measured progress, and relied on proven, data-driven methods. There was no guesswork, no panic, just grounded confidence earned through intentional effort.

Modern life wires your brain for quick dopamine hits, from smartphone notifications to processed foods, everything is designed for short-term rewards. But you can wire it back.

I've found that tracking everything and gamifying the process works incredibly well. I experiment with short runs to push my VO_2 max, test supplements, adjust meal timing, and fine-tune my evening wind-down routine. I closely monitor my recovery. Every check-in provides immediate data, actionable feedback, and a dopamine boost for all the right reasons.

It starts by making your progress visible. You track your wins, experiment intentionally, adjust your strategies, and reinforce positive behaviors. Habit tracking closes the feedback loop, helping you clearly see cause and effect.

The Hawthorne Effect further amplifies this: people naturally improve their behavior when they know they're being observed. When you record your meals, workouts, or sleep, you become both observer and participant. Visibility creates immediate accountability. You see the direct impact of good and bad choices, and improvement becomes inevitable.

Track your meals, fine-tune your nutrition, and watch your energy levels stabilize. You can't optimize what you don't measure, and most people are guessing…poorly:

Over 85% of Americans believe their diet is healthier than it actually is.

On average, studies show people underestimate calorie intake by 400–600 calories daily.

Fewer than 1 in 4 adults accurately estimate their daily caloric needs.

Start tracking your food. Use an app like *MyFitnessPal* or simply write it down. Log everything you eat. Visibility builds accountability, and accountability drives meaningful change.

Weigh in smarter. Use a smart scale that measures your actual body composition. Most people rely on outdated metrics like BMI, which can't differentiate muscle from fat. Advanced smart scales give clearer, more accurate insights into your health (and seriously, don't forget to weigh in!):

- **Body Fat Percentage**: The proportion of your body weight from fat. Essential for overall health, but excess body fat, especially around your organs, raises risks for heart disease, diabetes, and inflammation.

- **Muscle Mass**: The total weight of muscles in your body, reflecting strength, metabolism, and overall resilience.

- **Visceral Fat**: Deep internal fat surrounding vital organs; high levels strongly correlate with chronic illnesses like heart disease and type 2 diabetes.

- **Subcutaneous Fat**: Fat stored just beneath your skin, affecting your appearance but generally less harmful to your health than visceral fat.

- **Lean Body Mass**: The total weight of your body, excluding fat, including muscles, bones, organs, and water. Higher lean mass typically indicates better fitness and metabolic health.

- **Skeletal Mass**: The total weight of your bones, helping you monitor bone health and density over time.

While these measurements aren't always exact, they offer reliable trends and reveal exactly how your daily habits affect your body over time. Pairing your scale with intuitive apps, such as Hume, makes visualizing progress easy and motivating. Each measurement turns into a positive reinforcement of disciplined actions, reinforcing your commitment to long-term health.

Look at the Trends. Once you're tracking consistently, sometimes it helps to zoom out. Getting a new tracker or using a wearable for the first time can be overwhelming. It buzzes, flashes, and tracks metrics you've never thought about. It spits out numbers, graphs, sleep stages, recovery scores, heart rate zones, step counts, and VO_2 max estimates. You might feel like you're failing before you even start.

That's normal.

Take time to review all the features, watch tutorial videos, play around, and learn what each metric means and how to optimize it. It's okay if it takes a while to understand how it all connects. The goal isn't to be perfect every day; it's to build awareness and consistency over time.

Some days, your recovery score will be low. Some nights, your sleep will be garbage. That doesn't mean you're failing. What matters is the trend. Zoom out.

I like to review my data every few weeks and especially every few months, comparing trends in recovery, sleep quality, resting heart rate, and activity levels. That's where the real story lives. That's where progress hides.

Low time preference means zooming out. Just like with Bitcoin, a single bad night or off day doesn't define the trend. Progress takes time. What matters is the direction you're heading.

See a few of my Apple Watch and Hume trend screenshots on the next pages covering the past 6+ months (Figure 3 and 4).

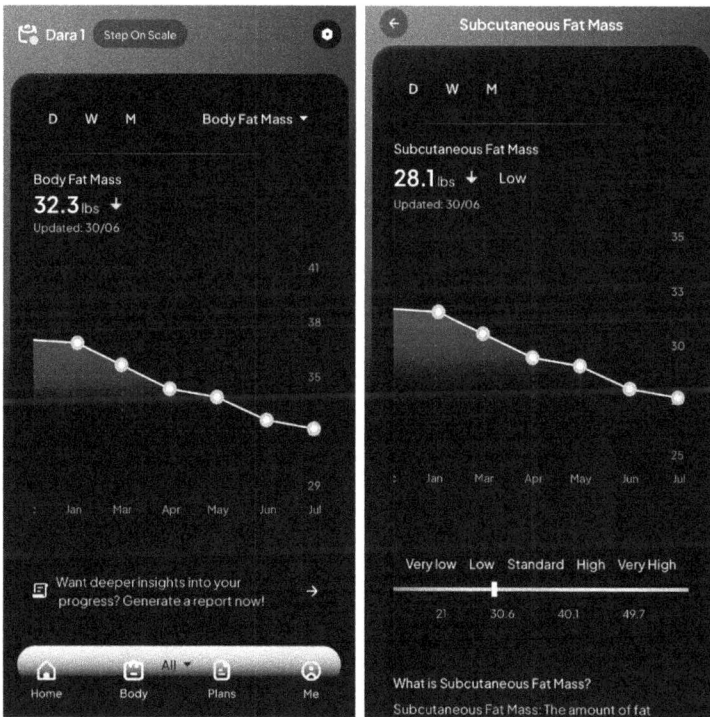

Figure 3: Body Fat Mass and Subcutaneous Fat Mass trends, measured using the Hume Smart Scale App.

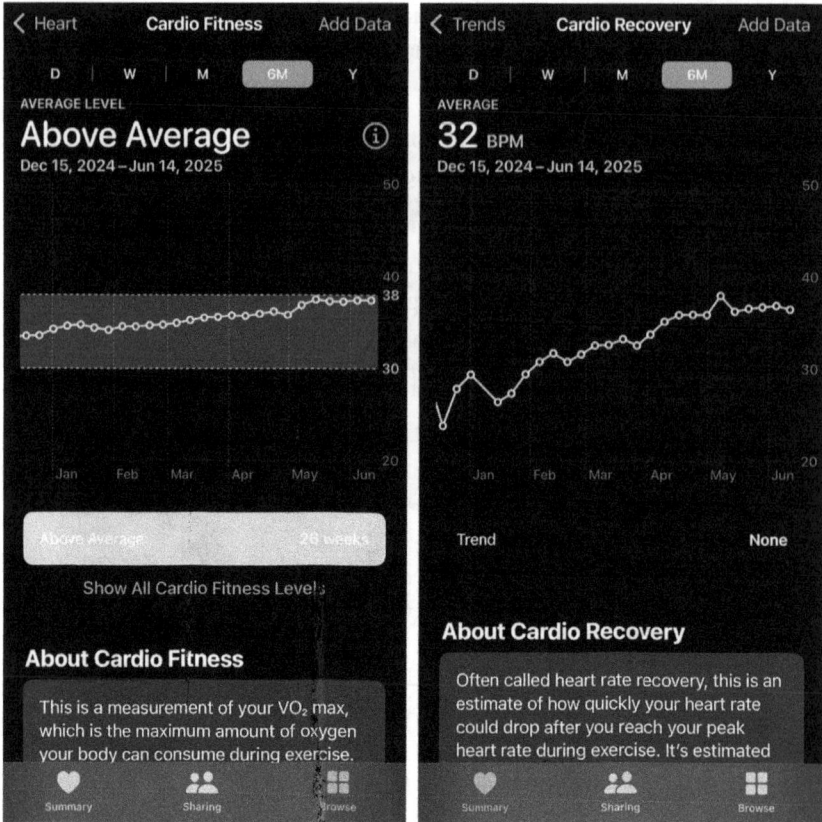

Figure 4: Trends for Cardio Fitness (VO₂ max) and Cardio Recovery (1-minute Heart Rate Recovery) from Apple Watch Fitness App.

Track your sleep, experiment with routines, and watch your recovery improve. We'll dive deeper into this in Chapter 6.

Track your workouts with your wearable. Find a workout or training app that clicks for you, experimenting until you discover what keeps you engaged. Personally, I aim for 2-3 resistance training sessions per week, around 3 HIIT workouts, and consistently average at least 10,000 steps daily. Exercise doesn't have to be boring, and you don't need to trap yourself in a gym. Do something you genuinely enjoy. I make sure to get out for at least one big hike per week, regularly ice skate, and go rock climbing. Find your thing, have fun, and build a habit that sticks.

One simple tool I highly recommend is a pull-up bar. You don't need anything fancy; your own body weight is plenty to build serious strength and resilience. Even if you can't do a pull-up yet, just hanging from the bar is great for your grip strength, posture, and spine. Add leg lifts or knee raises while hanging, and you'll build your core faster than any sit-up or crunch routine out there.

One of the most powerful metrics for optimizing workouts is tracking cardio **heart rate zones**. Your heart rate provides immediate, personalized feedback on your intensity, effort, and physiological response. By training in different heart rate zones, you precisely target specific health and fitness goals, from aerobic endurance to peak performance.

Here's how the five cardio zones break down:

Zone 1 (50–60% max heart rate)
Light Activity, Recovery & Warm-up.
Barely exerting yourself, easily holding a full conversation. Ideal for active recovery days and gentle warm-ups.

Zone 2 (60–70% max heart rate)
Aerobic Base, Endurance, Fat Burning.
Comfortable enough to maintain conversation. Perfect for cardiovascular fitness, mitochondrial function, and fat burning that's strongly linked to improved longevity.

Zone 3 (70–80% max heart rate)
Aerobic Conditioning, Moderate Intensity.
Speaking becomes challenging. Great for moderate cardio sessions that boost aerobic power and lactate threshold.

Zone 4 (80–90% max heart rate)
High-Intensity, Lactate Threshold, Performance.
Talking limited to short phrases. Enhances your ability to sustain high-intensity efforts, increasing speed, strength, and endurance.

Zone 5 (90–100% max heart rate)
Maximum Effort, Anaerobic Capacity, Speed.
Near-maximal effort. Intense intervals rapidly build fitness, anaerobic capacity, and improve VO_2 max.

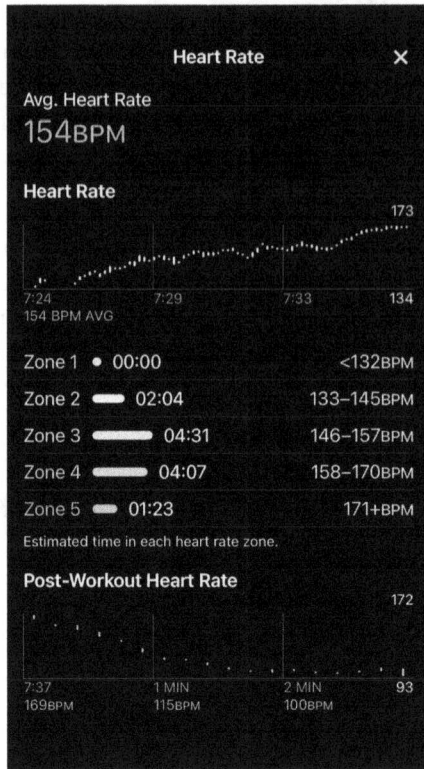

Figure 5: Apple Watch Heart Rate Zones and Recovery

Tracking these zones is straightforward with wearables like an Apple Watch (Figure 5), Fitbit, Garmin, Whoop, or Oura Ring. Most trackers automatically estimate your maximum heart rate (220 minus your age is a common starting point). Your tracker calculates personalized zones and provides live feedback during workouts, allowing precise targeting of your desired intensity.

In reality, something like a hike can check all the boxes: resistance training, HIIT, cardio zones, and steps. Here's how I integrate these metrics on hikes:

- **Run the hills:** Quickly raises heart rate into Zone 3 or Zone 4 (HIIT).

- **At the top:** Perform squats, push-ups, and lunges, which engage muscles with bodyweight resistance training.

- **A 4–5 mile hike:** Typically hits your 10,000-step goal, predominantly in Zone 2 for sustained aerobic endurance and fat burning.

All this tracking: steps, heart-rate zones, and resistance training make workouts engaging and rewarding. I love looking at my watch during a run and noticing when I'm right on the edge between zones, pushing myself just a little further to hit the next one. Measuring your progress transforms exercise into a motivating, personalized challenge. Clear feedback reinforces good habits, supports low time preference, and helps you stack meaningful victories.

That's how you future-proof your mind, body, and life: by building reliable, data-backed systems and habits that your future self will thank you for.

"Let It Rot" and the Crisis of Meaning

In my first book, *Intro to Bitcoin: Hope for a Better World*, I wrote about China's rising Bai Lan "Let it Rot" culture, a younger generation rejecting hustle, ambition, and long-term planning because they no longer see a future worth fighting for.

This goes deeper than laziness or a lack of motivation. It's rooted in despair.

Why work toward a future that feels hopeless, one defined by declining health, financial decay, and broken systems working against you? Why sacrifice today when tomorrow feels meaningless?

This crisis of meaning isn't unique to China. It's global. You see it in burnout, apathy, and entire generations disconnected from purpose. In the U.S., it's called "quiet quitting," where people show up to their jobs but mentally check out. In Japan, about 2% of the population aged 15 to 64 have become hikikomori, withdrawing from society and isolating themselves at home, often for years. Like China's "Let it Rot" culture, these trends highlight a global rise in nihilism: when traditional systems fail to offer meaningful futures, people simply stop participating.

But Bitcoin fundamentally shifts this mindset. So does focusing on healthspan and lifespan.

Both carry the same powerful message: *the future is real, it matters, and it's absolutely worth preparing for.*

When you commit to stacking for the long term, whether sats, strength, or sleep, you stop chasing temporary highs and numbing distractions. You begin building something authentic, tangible, and lasting. You move forward deliberately with clarity and purpose.

In doing so, you reclaim meaning. You reject nihilism and embrace ownership.

Low time preference is a hopeful way of living, intentionally building toward a meaningful future through patience and proof of work.

Every day, I ask myself:

"What habits am I stacking today that my future self will thank me for?"

That's the long game.

Low Time Preference Golden Milk Recipe

A warming, anti-inflammatory blend rooted in ancient tradition, perfect for your evening wind-down or caffeine-free mornings.

Ingredients:

- 1 cup unsweetened almond, oat, or coconut milk

- ½ tsp turmeric

- ¼ tsp ground ginger (or ½ inch fresh)

- Pinch of cinnamon

- Pinch of black pepper (for turmeric absorption)

- Optional: ¼ tsp cardamom or nutmeg

- Optional: 1 tsp maple syrup or raw honey

- Optional adaptogens: ¼ tsp ashwagandha or reishi

Instructions:

Gently warm milk on the stove. Whisk in spices until fully dissolved. Strain if using fresh ginger. Pour into your favorite mug and sip slowly.

This is low time preference in liquid form: calming, restorative, and designed to satisfy your cravings while nourishing your future self.

Bitcoin DCA Stacking Strategy: A Low Time Preference Recipe

DCA stands for **Dollar Cost Averaging.** It means investing a fixed amount of money at regular intervals, regardless of price. Over time, this smooths out volatility and removes emotion from the process. Instead of trying to time the market, you build a position with consistency and discipline.

Build long-term wealth through steady action. No hype. No guessing. Just consistency. Set it and forget it.

Ingredients:

- Automated stacking services (Strike, Swan Bitcoin, River, Cash App)

- Secure hardware wallet (Bitkey, Foundation Passport, Trezor, Cold Card, Seedsigner)

Instructions:

1. Choose your frequency for stacking Bitcoin. Consistency matters most.

2. Decide your fixed fiat investment amount for each interval.

3. Automate stacking with a trusted service for disciplined investing.

4. Regularly transfer your Bitcoin to a secure hardware wallet to safeguard against external entropy. (I recommend moving at least 1 million sats at a time to avoid dust-sized fragments that may be harder to spend later)

This isn't about timing the market or chasing gains. It's about showing up, stacking over time, and trusting the process. DCA is long-term thinking.

Low Time Preference Fitness Recipes

Train your body like you HODL: with consistency, intention, and long-term rewards.

Not all wearables estimate VO_2 max or recovery metrics. Even when they do, the data can be inconsistent. Lab tests with treadmills and ECG-grade monitors are the gold standard, but these simple, time-tested field tests offer accurate baselines and a way to track real progress over time. Think of them as physical "proof of work" checkpoints, hard to fake, easy to verify.

VO₂ Max Recipe: The 12-Minute Cooper Test

A reliable, low-tech way to estimate your aerobic capacity and cardiovascular endurance.

What It Measures

VO_2 max reflects how much oxygen your body can use during peak effort. Higher scores are linked to better cardiovascular health, stronger endurance, and a lower risk of chronic disease (Tables 1 and 2).

A lab test with a mask and treadmill is the gold standard. But if you don't have access to that, the Cooper Test offers a reliable estimate you can repeat anytime.

Ingredients:

- A flat track or GPS-measurable route

- A timer (watch or phone)

- A way to measure distance in miles

- Your full effort

Instructions:

1. Warm up for 5–10 minutes

2. Set a timer for 12 minutes

3. Run as far as you can—keep the pace hard but steady

4. Record your total distance in miles, rounded to two decimal places (e.g. 1.42 miles)

55

Calculate Your VO₂ Max:
Use this version of the Cooper formula for miles:
VO_2 max = $(35.97 \times miles) - 11.29$

Example:
If you run 1.50 miles in 12 minutes:
VO_2 max = $(35.97 \times 1.50) - 11.29 \approx 42.7$ ml/kg/min

VO₂ Max Categories (General Guidelines)

Table 1: VO2 Max Classification – Males

Age	20-29	30-39	40-49	50-59	60-69	70-79
Superior (95th)	55.4	54	52.5	48.9	45.7	42.1
Excellent (80th)	55.1	48.3	46.4	43.4	39.5	36.7
Good (60th)	45.4	44	42.4	39.2	35.5	32.2
Fair (40th)	41.7	40.5	38.5	35.6	32.3	29.4
Poor (<40th)	41.6	40.4	38.4	35.5	32.2	29.3

Table 2: VO2 Max Classification – Females

Age	20-29	30-39	40-49	50-59	60-69	70-79
Superior (95th)	49.6	47.4	45.3	41.1	37.8	36.7
Excellent (80th)	43.9	42.4	39.7	36.7	33.0	30.9
Good (60th)	39.5	37.8	36.3	33.0	30.0	28.1
Fair (40th)	36.1	34.4	33	30.1	27.5	25.9
Poor (<40th)	36.0	34.3	32.9	30.0	27.4	25.9

These tables can help you interpret your VO_2 Max results from the 12-Minute Cooper Test or any fitness tracker that estimates VO_2 Max.

How To Improve VO₂ Max:

• Do more zone 2 cardio (easy runs, long hikes, cycling, where you can still talk)

- Mix in HIIT (high intensity interval training) once or twice a week (e.g., 4 rounds of 4 minutes hard effort, 3 minutes rest)

- Get quality sleep

- Walk more

- Avoid chronic stress and ultra-processed food

- Retest every 4–8 weeks

Why It Matters:

The higher your VO_2 max, the more energy your body can produce and use efficiently. It doesn't just show up in workouts; it shows up in your ability to recover, focus, and move well as you age. It won't improve overnight, but it's worth building toward. More capacity means more options, more resilience, more life.

That's low time preference in action.

HRR Recipe: 3-Minute Heart Rate Recovery Test

Optimize your recovery to enhance cardiovascular health and longevity.

Overview:

Heart Rate Recovery (HRR) shows how quickly your heart rate drops after intense exercise. It's a powerful signal of cardiovascular health and nervous system adaptability. A faster recovery means your system is adaptable. It knows how to push hard, then settle efficiently.

Some wearables track this automatically, often labeled as "cardio recovery" or "recovery rate." If yours does, use the data. If not, this 3-minute test gives you a simple way to measure and track your recovery over time (Table 3).

This is how you apply low time preference to your health. You build capacity through consistent habits and track progress that compounds slowly.

Ingredients:

- A heart rate monitor (smartwatch, chest strap, or pulse-taking skill)

- Stopwatch or timer

- Open space or a cardio machine

- A quiet spot to sit or stand afterward

Instructions:

1. **Warm up** for 5–10 minutes with light movement.

2. **Go hard** for 2–3 minutes, run, cycle, climb stairs, enough to reach at least 85–95% of your max heart rate.

3. **Stop immediately** and sit down. Don't walk around. Let your body fully rest.

4. **Record** your heart rate at four points:

   - 0 minutes (peak HR)

   - 1 minute

   - 2 minutes

   - 3 minutes

5. **Calculate** your Heart Rate Recovery (HRR):

  • **1-min HRR** = Peak HR − HR at 1 min

  • **2-min HRR** = Peak HR − HR at 2 min

  • **3-min HRR** = Peak HR − HR at 3 min

Example:
Let's say your peak heart rate hits **160 bpm** after exertion.

1. After 1 minute: **132 bpm** -->**1-min HRR = 160 − 132 = 28 bpm**

2. After 2 minutes: **120 bpm** --> **2-min HRR = 40 bpm**

3. After 3 minutes: **110 bpm** --> **3-min HRR = 50 bpm**

Table 3: Heart Rate Recovery Levels

Percentile	HRR1 (1 min)	HRR2 (2 min)	HRR3 (3 min)	Category
Elite – 95th	41 bpm	83 bpm	100 bpm	Exceptional recovery
Elite – 75th	28 bpm	68 bpm	88 bpm	Strong recovery
Elite – 50th	21 bpm	59 bpm	83 bpm	Above average
Population – 50th	23 bpm	58 bpm	82 bpm	Average
Population – 25th	17 bpm	48 bpm	74 bpm	Below average
Population – 10th	11 bpm	40 bpm	68 bpm	Poor recovery
Population – 5th	9 bpm	31 bpm	62 bpm	High risk

Tips to Improve HRR:

  • Prioritize aerobic training 3–5 times a week

  • Eat whole, anti-inflammatory foods

  • Hydrate consistently

- Go to bed on time and aim for 7-8 hours of quality sleep

- Take walking breaks throughout the day

- Practice stress management (breathwork, meditation, walks, creative flow)

- Limit alcohol, as it weakens recovery and disrupts sleep

- Reduce stimulant use (especially caffeine late in the day)

Why It Matters:

HRR reflects how well your body recovers from stress. It shows whether your system knows how to shift gears and reset. That ability carries over into how you sleep, how you handle pressure, and how well you adapt over time. You no longer need to guess whether your recovery is improving. You can measure it.

Part 2

Securing Your Future: The Bitcoin and Longevity Blueprint

Chapter 4

The Broken Financial System: Why Bitcoin is the Answer

I was eighteen years old in the summer of 2008, having just graduated from high school and anxiously awaiting the start of college in the fall. The air felt heavy that year, and not just from the stifling August humidity in Ohio. Something else hung thick with tension, uncertainty, subtle hints that something was deeply wrong, even if I couldn't yet name it.

Earlier that spring, as my senior year was wrapping up, gas prices surged from around $2 a gallon to over $4.20 a gallon. I vividly recall sitting in the parking lot of the grocery store where I worked part-time, having just gotten a raise from $5.15 to $6.85 an hour (due to an increase in minimum wage). Yet that extra $1.70 per hour felt meaningless as I frantically calculated: could I afford gas to drive to my college classes, get to work, and still eat something today? I had started attending college classes early, taking advantage of a free program offered to high school students, but now even that privilege felt just out of reach.

Throughout that summer, words like "subprime mortgages," "derivatives," and "bailouts" flashed across television screens, cryptic and abstract to someone whose immediate concern was daily survival. But the truth was, those headlines barely touched our everyday struggles. We were already poor and financially unstable, economic downturns didn't make a significant difference because things had always been hard. While job losses did ripple through our community, the crisis itself felt distant, a problem for people who had something to lose. Still, watching banks and big institutions receive massive bailouts while ordinary families lost homes and livelihoods felt profoundly unfair.

Witnessing that deep unfairness planted questions inside me, questions about a system that felt rigged, questions that quietly grew and eventually led me to search for something better.

Fast forward to 2020. History didn't just repeat; it intensified. COVID brought the world to a standstill, and in response, governments unleashed trillions of dollars into existence overnight. Stocks soared, home prices surged, yet quietly, beneath these booming markets, the cost of groceries, rent, and other essentials crept higher, too. We didn't get to vote on printing that money; we had no say in diluting our savings. Yet, we were the ones paying higher grocery bills, higher rent, and watching our savings quietly erode.

This dynamic is known as the **Cantillon Effect**, where newly created money disproportionately benefits those who receive it first, typically large financial institutions, banks with preferential access to low-interest capital, and wealthy investors who leverage easy credit to accumulate appreciating assets. It's a hidden advantage for the few at the expense of the many.

Fiat currency, the money issued by governments and accepted as normal, is how most people store the value of their time and labor. That's when I truly grasped a simple, powerful truth: *Inflation is time theft.* Fiat money silently erodes the value we've earned, stealing from us every day. To genuinely secure your future, you need to recognize the money trap we've inherited and understand why Bitcoin is the best tool we have to escape it.

The Long Road to Bitcoin

Money has always been imperfect. Humans have tried seashells, beads, giant stones, and precious metals, each attempt solving some problems while creating others. I remember reading about early North American settlers trading Wampum beads (Figure 6), which were valuable due to their scarcity, until Europeans flooded markets with cheap, mass-produced beads. Overnight, the once-valuable Wampum became worthless.

Half a world away, on Yap Island, villagers used massive, immovable stone disks called Rai stones as money (Figure 6), their value secured by the difficulty of production and scarcity. When Europeans arrived with iron tools, easily creating more stones, scarcity collapsed along with their monetary value. These stories made me realize how easily money could lose its value when its scarcity is compromised.

Even gold, historically humanity's strongest candidate for stable money, had flaws (Figure 7). Roman emperors shaved bits off coins or diluted them with cheaper metals to fund their wars, quietly robbing citizens of their wealth. Later, banks began issuing more paper certificates than they had gold, inflating away value and distorting trust.

Figure 6: Wampum Beads and Rai Stone (Photorealistic images created in Image GPT by Erin E. Malone).

Figure 7: Variations of Gold as money (Photorealistic image created in Image GPT by Erin E. Malone).

And then came fiat, money backed by nothing but government decree. It promised flexibility but delivered disasters, like Germany's hyperinflation in the Weimar Republic, where wheelbarrows full of cash were needed to buy basic food (Figure 8). The way fiat currencies are designed makes them ripe for manipulation, tools of centralized power. When you have direct access to currency issuance (think unlimited money printing), the temptation to manipulate it is just too strong. History has shown that every fiat currency eventually collapses in value.

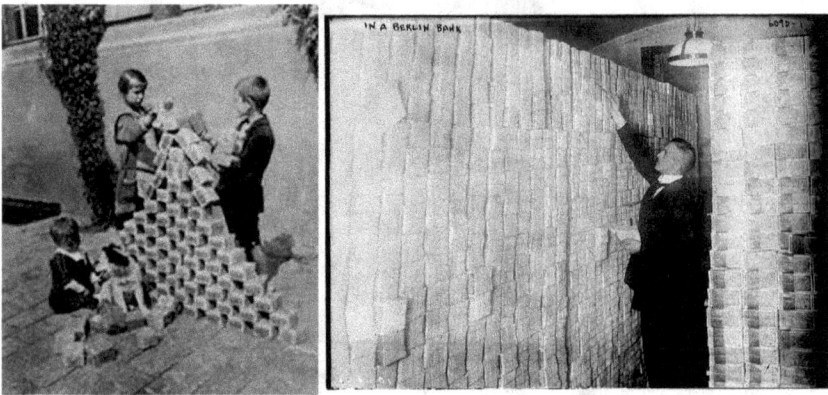

Figure 8: (Left) Hyperinflation in Germany, 1923 (Unknown Author, Wikimedia Commons). (Right) Money stacked in a Berlin bank (Bain News Service, Wikimedia Commons).

"If you debase the currency, you debase the country."
- *Masaru Hayami, Governor of the Bank of Japan (1998–2003)*

Bitcoin: Humanity's Monetary Evolution

Bitcoin didn't just appear one day. It emerged from decades of cryptographic research, carefully crafted to avoid every historical pitfall money faced. Bitcoin combined gold's scarcity and durability with the portability and security of digital technology. Capped forever at 21 million coins, Bitcoin's supply can't be inflated by politicians or banks. It's money immune to manipulation, censorship, and decay, secured transparently by a global network anyone can verify.

I first discovered Bitcoin when I began questioning the subtle erosion of my savings… and my future. Bitcoin felt different. It felt fair. It represented a fundamental shift away from money that stole my time, toward money that protected it.

Mining Reward: BIG B or little b?

Fun fact: A lowercase "bitcoin" (b) refers to the asset, while an uppercase "Bitcoin" (B) refers to the network.

The Fiat Trap: Quietly Stealing Your Future

When I looked closely at historical data, the theft became painfully clear. In 1971, the year the U.S. officially went off the gold standard, the average U.S. home cost around $27,000. By 2025, that same home soared to nearly $497,700, a staggering 1,743% increase. Yet, this wasn't just about homes becoming more valuable; it was the dollar steadily losing its worth.

Measured in bitcoin, home prices told a radically different story (Figure 9):

Bitcoin Needed to Buy the Average U.S. Home (2016, 2020, 2024)

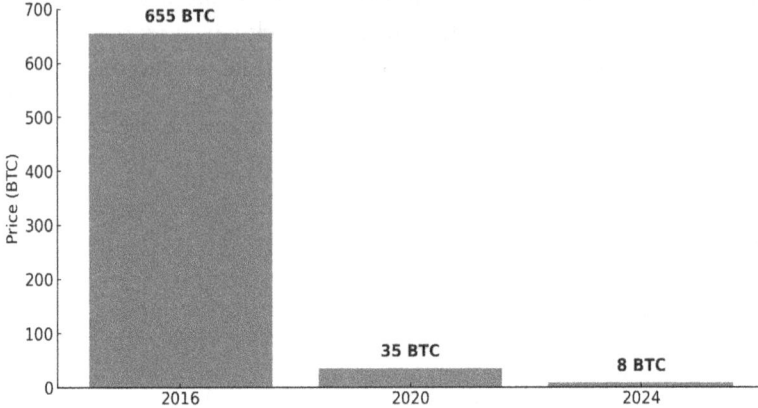

Figure 9: Amount of bitcoin needed to buy a house from 2016- 2024. Created by Erin E. Malone.

In 2016, the average home cost about 655 bitcoin or $339,300.

By 2020, that dropped sharply to around 35 bitcoin or $375,000.

In 2024, it further plummeted to just 8 bitcoin or $519,700.

This contrast illustrates bitcoin's true power: while fiat prices spiral out of control, bitcoin preserves your purchasing power and protects your time from the theft of inflation.

The Broader Implications

The fiat system disproportionately favors those closest to newly created money, reinforcing inequality and shrinking opportunities for everyday individuals. By the time new money reaches ordinary people, inflation has already set in and quietly eroded their purchasing power. Meanwhile, prices for essential assets and services such as homes and healthcare rise faster than wages, steadily shrinking opportunities for everyday individuals to achieve financial stability.

Earlier, we briefly discussed how not all success comes from proof of work. This problem is amplified in our current economic system. When zombie corporations, unprofitable companies propped up by cheap debt and easy money, thrive without delivering real value, it distorts genuine innovation and progress. Instead of rewarding real effort, this easy-money environment incentivizes short-term thinking, speculation, and complacency. Bitcoin breaks this cycle by reintroducing true proof of work into money itself, aligning incentives directly with productivity, rewarding value creation rather than financial engineering.

> "It is well enough that people of the nation do not understand our banking and monetary system, for if they did, I believe there would be a revolution before tomorrow morning."
>
> *- Henry Ford*

Mining Reward: Got Bitcoin?

All fiat currencies eventually trend toward zero. Since the creation of the Federal Reserve in 1913, the U.S. dollar has lost roughly 98% of its purchasing power. Bitcoin preserves your value, choose wisely.

Bitcoin: Your Path to Financial Sovereignty

Bitcoin offers a fundamentally different approach to money, one explicitly designed to address all the historical shortcomings of traditional monetary systems. By allocating a portion of your savings into Bitcoin, you can shield your financial future from the inherent weaknesses and manipulation of fiat currencies.

Bitcoin's true revolution is protecting your savings, your purchasing power, and your future. Its fixed supply, decentralized nature, transparency, portability, censorship resistance, divisibility, and fungibility create a financial foundation immune to fiat's flaws:

- **Scarcity:** Bitcoin is limited to 21 million coins, protecting against inflation and monetary dilution. Unlike fiat currency, no government or institution can produce more.

- **Decentralization:** Bitcoin is not controlled by any central authority or government, removing the risks of manipulation, confiscation, and political interference.

- **Transparency and Verifiability (Immutability):** Every transaction on Bitcoin's blockchain is permanently recorded and publicly verifiable. This immutable ledger prevents fraud, coin clipping, or manipulation, problems historically seen in precious metals and fiat currencies.

- **Portability:** Bitcoin can be sent instantly and securely around the globe without physical limitations or borders. It solves gold's portability issues and eliminates risks associated with transporting or storing physical assets.

- **Censorship Resistance (Aligned Economic Incentives):** No entity can block, reverse, or censor Bitcoin transactions. Attempting to censor or manipulate Bitcoin for personal or political gain directly contradicts the network's economic incentives and typically results in financial losses. Miners and network participants are financially rewarded for maintaining integrity, openness, and neutrality. This built-in economic alignment ensures that the Bitcoin network naturally resists censorship and manipulation.

- **Divisibility and Fungibility:** Each Bitcoin divides into 100 million smaller units called "satoshis," allowing precise, flexible transactions. Bitcoin units are interchangeable (fungible), ensuring seamless global usability and trade.

A Deflationary World

We live in a world defined by exponential technological advancement. Every year, humans become increasingly productive, leveraging innovation to achieve more with less: fewer resources, less time, and reduced effort. Technology should naturally drive prices lower by making goods and services cheaper and easier to produce. Yet, despite this ongoing progress, the cost of living continues to rise, pushing everyday necessities further out of reach. Why does this paradox exist? Why are we more productive than ever, yet working harder just to maintain our standard of living? The root lies in our broken monetary system. Our current fiat currency is engineered for inflation, quietly eroding the value of our time and labor even as technology tries to pull prices down. This mismatch traps us in a perpetual struggle, preventing the natural benefits of innovation from reaching us.

(Excerpted and adapted from my book, *Intro to Bitcoin: Hope for a Better World*.)

> It's Friday night in 2004, and you just snagged the latest DVD release at Blockbuster. You wait in line, hand the cashier your money, verify you don't have any overdue charges, and then…freedom! You drive home and pop that baby in the DVD player. What a time to be alive.

> How much the world has changed.

> Our media became digitized. Smartphones dominated, app stores emerged, and streaming movies became the norm. Books, music, movies, and shows transitioned to digital formats, accessible from any smart device. Accessing media became instant, and costs dropped dramatically. You could pay $15/month for Netflix and instantly watch thousands of movies without leaving your home.

> You no longer have the cost of manufacturing DVDs, packaging, distribution, or running physical stores. The time and money spent driving to rent and return movies disappeared.

> Technology increases productivity, naturally causing prices to fall. Books that once filled entire libraries now fit on a Kindle or iPad. Tools like compasses or calculators are now free apps on your phone.

> Yet fiat *inflation* distorts these deflationary gains. Productivity improves, but living expenses somehow still increase. People work harder just to keep pace.

> Bitcoin emerges as a beacon of hope in this scenario, offering a deflationary money for the deflationary world that technology brings. If we saved the fruits of our labor in bitcoin, our money would more accurately mirror our advancements in productivity, enhancing purchasing power and the overall quality of life technology brings.

Shouldn't we have a money that aligns with the natural deflationary trends of technological progress? And shouldn't our money be digital in this new digitized age, offering access anytime and from anywhere, enabling instant, borderless transactions? Why do we need to rely on intermediaries such as governments and banks to be our "blockbusters?" Why do they control the supply of money? Bitcoin cuts out the middlemen. Bitcoin is a technology that increases productivity and puts the power and control back in the hands of the user.

Bitcoin is designed to pass these deflationary gains directly to users, preserving and amplifying purchasing power. This alignment between Bitcoin's design and technology's natural deflation reshapes not just money, but society itself, empowering you to leverage innovation to build a better life in a world increasingly shaped by AI and technological advancement.

True Financial Sovereignty

Choosing bitcoin isn't about chasing short-term profits or riding speculative waves. It's about protecting your savings from inflation, manipulation, and systemic risk. Bitcoin replaces blind trust with transparent mathematics, cryptography, and decentralized networks. By adopting bitcoin, you're reclaiming your financial power, today, tomorrow, and future generations.

Mining Reward: Proof of Humility

Understanding Bitcoin starts with humility. Let go of old assumptions about money and stay open to learning something new. Bitcoin is an ego test, not an intelligence test.

Why Bitcoin Preserves Time

Every dollar saved represents hours, days, or even decades of your life spent working. Inflation quietly steals those hours away, gradually eroding the value of your past efforts. Bitcoin flips this dynamic, offering money specifically engineered to preserve the true value of your time. With bitcoin, you can allocate more resources toward living longer, healthier, and more fulfilling years.

Bitcoin's defining feature is scarcity. Fiat currency can be printed endlessly, but bitcoin's total supply is capped forever at 21 million coins. No political decision, economic upheaval, or institutional intervention can alter this limit, as it's hard-coded into Bitcoin's source code and enforced by thousands of nodes running worldwide. This built-in scarcity transforms bitcoin into a reliable store of value, much like digital gold, but with significantly greater portability and security.

The constant dilution of fiat currency distorts our sense of value. Prices rise, wages stagnate, and our future security quietly diminishes. Bitcoin clarifies this distortion, serving as an immutable measuring stick that reveals the hidden damage of inflation. Cars have actually become cheaper to produce over time, thanks to technological advancements, automation, and more efficient manufacturing processes. Yet, in fiat terms, prices have risen significantly. In 2016, buying an average new car required approximately 60 bitcoin. By 2020, the same purchase only required four bitcoin, and by 2024, just one bitcoin was needed (Table 4).

This isn't because cars became cheaper or bitcoin became more abundant; it's because bitcoin preserved purchasing power, while fiat currency steadily lost its value. Priced in bitcoin, everything from education to healthcare to food becomes steadily more affordable, aligning closely with the true cost reductions driven by technology. Bitcoin may be volatile in the short term when priced in fiat, but zooming out reveals its true strength even over a four-year horizon. Bitcoin restores transparency and fairness to how we value our time and labor, making sure the effort we put in today will retain its value into the future.

Table 4: Average Cost in USD of New Cars From 2016-2024

Year	Average New Car Price (USD)	Bitcoin Needed
2016	$34,077	60 BTC
2020	$38,940	4 BTC
2024	$48,401	1 BTC

Mining Reward: Inflation Shortens Lifespan

Constantly working harder just to maintain your purchasing power creates chronic stress and uncertainty. Studies show persistent financial stress directly reduces healthspan and lifespan, increasing your risk of heart disease, obesity, sleep disorders, and depression. Protecting your wealth with Bitcoin safeguards your finances, long-term health, and peace of mind.

The Debt Spiral

As of mid-2025, the U.S. national debt has surpassed $37 trillion. Interest payments alone now exceed the country's entire defense budget. This endless borrowing quietly erodes your purchasing power and financial security. Like paying off a Visa card with your Mastercard, the cycle of debt spirals deeper, continually weakening the dollar and stealing time from your future.

By 2030, the Congressional Budget Office predicts annual interest payments could surpass $1 trillion, forcing the government to print even more money just to pay the interest. Meanwhile, Congress regularly raises the debt ceiling, and massive spending bills push us deeper into debt. At this point, there's no realistic way out. By 2034, annual interest payments are predicted to surpass $2.2 trillion, more than doubling current levels. Interest payments alone would consume nearly 30% of government revenue, becoming the second-largest federal expenditure, surpassing Medicare and defense spending. As interest payments rise, the government will be forced to print even more money to cover the interest, driving debt higher and accelerating an already dangerous spiral.

Humans have always been irresponsible with money creation. Every global superpower has eventually destroyed its currency through excessive money printing or manipulation, and history continues to repeat itself. More recently, Zimbabwe saw trillion-dollar bills become souvenirs. Argentina experienced three hyperinflationary crises within my lifetime alone. Venezuela, Lebanon, Turkey, and Sudan have also recently faced severe hyperinflation.

Despite being the global reserve currency, the U.S, is not immune. The collapse might take longer due to global dependence on the dollar, but eventually, the consequences of reckless money printing will be severe, especially for countries that rely on the dollar but have no control over its printing.

Since the 2008 financial crisis, the U.S. has been kicking the can down the road, printing money to patch holes instead of addressing the underlying issues. But this cycle can't last forever. Nothing stops this debt spiral within the current system.

You can watch this debt spiral unfold in real-time at USDebtClock.org.

Bitcoin offers the only real escape hatch. It's money that cannot be printed, manipulated, or devalued. When your currency preserves value instead of destroying it, you regain control of your time, wealth, and future.

Why Altcoins Repeat Fiat's Mistakes

Bitcoin uniquely addresses the historical weaknesses of money, yet today, there are over 30,000 cryptocurrency projects claiming superior solutions. Collectively known as "altcoins" (alternative coins to Bitcoin), these projects include well-known examples such as Ethereum, Dogecoin, Solana, and countless others. While often presented as innovative or superior alternatives to Bitcoin, most altcoins replicate the fundamental flaws of fiat currency: centralized control, unclear or shifting monetary policies, and vulnerability to inflation and manipulation.

For instance, Ethereum, the second-largest cryptocurrency by market cap, has experienced significant hacks within its broader ecosystem, such as the DAO hack in 2016 and the Ronin Network hack in 2022, and controversial **chain rollbacks**, undermining its core promise of immutability. Originally based on Proof of Work, Ethereum migrated to Proof of Stake, shifting control from computational power to wealth, effectively empowering the wealthiest holders. Approximately 70% of Ethereum's initial supply was **pre-mined**, primarily held by insiders and the Ethereum Foundation, creating extreme centralization. The Ethereum Foundation has repeatedly sold tokens at market peaks, disadvantaging ordinary investors. Additionally, running a full Ethereum node has become prohibitively expensive, further weakening its decentralization.

Dogecoin, initially created as a joke, continuously adds approximately 10,000 coins every minute to its supply, perpetually diluting its value and reinforcing a fiat-like inflation. It lacks meaningful network effects, with very few nodes or miners supporting its network, making it vulnerable and unstable.

Solana exemplifies extreme centralization. The network frequently goes offline due to technical failures and centralized points of failure. Its reliability is severely compromised, undermining trust and usability as a stable monetary instrument.

Many altcoins begin with significant "pre-mines," granting project creators and insiders disproportionate control. This closely mirrors the unfair advantage central banks and financial institutions hold in fiat systems. Additionally, their monetary policies frequently shift unpredictably, diluting their value and eroding trust. Unlike Bitcoin's fixed, transparent, and unchangeable supply limit of 21 million coins, altcoins are routinely prone to manipulation by developers and stakeholders.

Altcoins lack Bitcoin's robust network effects: global adoption, proven security, liquidity, and decentralization. Without these foundational strengths, altcoins predominantly serve as speculative assets rather than reliable monetary instruments.

Altcoins are often solutions looking for problems, technology experiments without clear real-world applications. Unlike Bitcoin, they fail to address monetary issues in a meaningful way. Many altcoin projects effectively operate as pump-and-dump schemes, enriching founders or early investors at the expense of ordinary participants. Leveraging marketing tactics, social media hype, and paid influencers, these projects inflate their coin's perceived value, creating the exit liquidity founders need to "dump" their coins for quick profits. They exploit "unit bias," the misconception that lower nominal prices imply greater investment potential, misleading people into believing they're "late" to Bitcoin. Investors often overlook critical metrics, such as total supply, market capitalization, and Bitcoin's substantial network effects, including widespread adoption, tens of thousands of globally distributed nodes that enforce consensus, and millions of miners collectively producing hundreds of **exahashes** per second to secure and validate every transaction.

Bitcoin stands uniquely apart. Meticulously crafted through decades of cryptographic research, it provides genuine resistance to manipulation, inflation, and centralization, all issues that continue to undermine altcoins. "Bitcoin, not crypto" has become a rallying cry among those who understand the deeper monetary revolution at play. Bitcoin is a robust, engineered solution addressing humanity's enduring monetary challenges, fundamentally different from other cryptocurrencies.

Bitcoin fixes the money. Everything else is noise.

Mining Reward: Carry Your Wealth Anywhere

Bitcoin allows you to secure your wealth in your mind. By memorizing a simple 12-word recovery phrase, you can discreetly transport your savings anywhere, even across borders. For refugees fleeing conflict or instability, this means protecting wealth from theft, confiscation, and inflation. Bitcoin provides security, financial freedom, and lasting hope.

Financial sovereignty means reclaiming your time and energy from broken systems. Inflation quietly erodes your savings, trapping you in survival mode and making proactive health feel unattainable. Bitcoin preserves your purchasing power, allowing you to invest in nutritious food, quality sleep, regular exercise, and preventive care. Taking control of your money allows you to take control of your health.

The Path to Financial Sovereignty: Cold Storage Recipe

Discovering Bitcoin and realizing it could protect my time was a revelation, but it was only half the journey. True financial freedom requires more than just holding Bitcoin; it means fully taking control of it. Leaving your Bitcoin on exchanges or with custodians might feel convenient, but it's fundamentally no different than trusting banks, leaving your assets vulnerable to hacks, mismanagement, or collapse.

Wallets (Signing Devices or Private Key Storage)

- **Hot Wallet:** A Bitcoin wallet connected directly to the internet, such as smartphone or computer applications. Hot wallets offer convenience and ease of use for everyday transactions, but come with higher risk due to online vulnerabilities.

- **Cold Wallet (Cold Storage):** A Bitcoin wallet that is completely offline and usually stored on specialized hardware devices. Keeping private keys offline significantly reduces hacking risks and online threats, making cold wallets the most secure method for long-term storage.

- **Hardware Wallet**: A physical device designed to securely store private keys offline, typically resembling USB drives or small digital devices. Hardware wallets are the most common form of cold storage.

- **Software Wallet:** A software application (usually on smartphones or computers) used to store and manage Bitcoin. Software wallets are hot wallets (connected to the internet), making them more vulnerable to hacks, malware, and other online threats since the private keys are stored digitally. Using a software wallet also involves trusting the software developer's security measures and integrity.

Single-Signature vs. Multisignature

- **Single-Signature (Single-Sig):** A wallet setup that requires only one private key (signature) to authorize transactions. Single-sig is simpler but has a single point of failure; if you lose your private key, you lose access to your Bitcoin.

- **Multisignature (Multisig):** A wallet setup requiring multiple private keys to authorize transactions, for example, needing 2 out of 3 keys.

Multisig increases security, reducing the risk of loss or theft by eliminating any single point of failure.

Why Cold Storage Matters

Think of cold storage as your personal vault, securely tucked away from any external risks. By holding your private keys offline, you safeguard your wealth from systemic failures, censorship, or confiscation. This isn't just about security; it's about stepping fully into your sovereignty, making sure your Bitcoin stays yours, permanently.

Taking Self-Custody Recipe: A Step-by-Step Guide

Below are some of the most trusted devices and methods among Bitcoiners. Every user is unique, so it's important to find the solution that best fits your comfort, security needs, and technical skill level. *Always do your own research*. Remember, your security is only as strong as your security practices; the devices themselves are just one part of maintaining sovereignty and protecting your Bitcoin. The following recommendations serve as a starting point for your self-custody journey.

Ingredients:

• Hardware wallet (single signature or multi-signature)

• Metal backup solution (steel plates or metal seed cards)

• Secure, offline storage location

• Reliable internet connection (for initial setup and transactions)

Instructions:

Step 1: Choose Your Wallet Type

• Single Signature Wallets (Beginner-Friendly, Secure)

  • **Foundation Passport:** User-friendly, air-gapped, Bitcoin-only wallet with advanced security.

  • **Trezor (Model T, Model One):** Easy to use, secure, open-source firmware.

  • **Blockstream Jade:** Cost-effective, open-source, supports multisig setups.

- **Coldcard:** High-security, air-gapped wallet for advanced users.

- **SeedSigner:** Open-source, DIY-style wallet offering complete transparency and customization.

- Multi-Signature Wallets (Enhanced Security, Redundancy)

  - **Bitkey:** Simplified multisig solution perfect for beginners, offering enhanced security without complexity or seed words to manage.

  - **Casa:** Intuitive management, robust recovery, and built-in inheritance planning.

  - **Unchained Capital:** Collaborative custody with full personal control, redundancy, and flexibility.

Step 2: Purchase Directly from the Manufacturer

- To avoid compromised devices, always order your hardware wallet from the official manufacturer's website. Also, beware of tampered packaging.

Step 3: Set Up Your Wallet

- Follow your device's initial setup instructions carefully.

- Generate your secure recovery phrase (typically 12 or 24 words).

- Write it down clearly on the provided recovery sheet.

- NEVER store your recovery phrase digitally.

Step 4: Secure Your Recovery Phrase

- Transfer your recovery phrase onto a metal backup solution to protect against fire, water, and physical damage.

- Store it securely in a safe, hidden, or off-site location.

Step 5: Transfer Your Bitcoin from Exchanges

- Generate a receiving address on your hardware wallet.

- First, send a small test amount to confirm everything works. Once it arrives, wipe your device and restore it using your recovery phrase to verify your backup is accurate.

- After confirming everything works, I like to send the test amount back to its original wallet.

- Then, withdraw the full amount to the verified hardware wallet address, carefully double-checking addresses, verifying at least the first and last five characters.

- This extra step ensures your **UTXOs**, the chunks of Bitcoin your wallet controls, are large enough to spend in the future.

Step 6: Regularly Verify and Update

- Keep your hardware wallet firmware updated.

- Periodically practice restoring your wallet with your recovery phrase to ensure familiarity and accuracy

Practical Tips

- Always verify addresses thoroughly before sending Bitcoin.

- Never share your private keys or recovery phrase. Legitimate services will never request these.

- Maintain good security hygiene, regular firmware updates, secure storage, and diligent verification practices.

- I recommend moving at least 1 million sats at a time to avoid dust-sized fragments that may be harder to spend later.

Self-custody is about reclaiming your time, autonomy, and freedom from a broken financial system. It's your path to true sovereignty.

Chapter 5

The Broken Healthcare System:
Why Longevity is in Your Hands

I've stopped outsourcing my health to doctors.

In early 2024, chronic back pain from ice skating plunged me into a health-care nightmare. For nearly a year, I bounced from my primary doctor, a spine specialist, multiple physical therapists, and a sports medicine doctor. Appointments were scheduled months apart, even though pain kept me awake nearly every night. Each specialist offered a new diagnosis, but no real solutions.

Visits to my primary doctor were especially frustrating. Whenever I asked detailed questions, whether about back pain or other health concerns, she immediately turned to her computer, typed my symptoms into WebMD, and read the results verbatim. Sometimes she'd even hand me a printout of the exact same page. Sitting there in disbelief, I thought: *How is this health-care? And why am I paying this much money for it?*

My husband endured a similar ordeal. Decades of repetitive technician work left him with chronic wrist pain and stiffness. For over a year and a half, he too was shuffled between specialists, therapists, and ineffective treatments. Like me, he was offered steroid injections and temporary fixes, but no genuine solutions. We were both caught in a loop of endless appointments, prescriptions, and frustration, with nothing that actually helped.

Every interaction with the medical system left me feeling powerless, con-fused, and financially drained. Bills arrived that I was assured were covered by insurance, yet somehow weren't. A few years earlier, a rollerblading accident sent me to the ER with eight stitches in my head. Despite having insurance, I ended up with a bill of over $3,000. Hidden fees, vague charges, and misleading coverage explanations always followed. Even more surprisingly, healthcare services often cost significantly less if you pay out of pocket without insurance. Yet we face penalties for not carrying insurance, insurance that rarely seems to fully cover anything anyway. The whole system feels intentionally confusing, as if someone profits directly from our uncertainty.

All these experiences confirmed a suspicion I'd held for a while: our healthcare system is fundamentally broken. It's expensive, inefficient, and reactive, constantly prioritizing short-term relief and billing codes over long-term prevention and genuine solutions. The misaligned priorities run so deep that even hospital food reflects this dysfunction. Last year, I witnessed a friend's mom hospitalized for months, regularly served Jell-O, sugary juices, and ultra-processed foods. She didn't have diabetes when she was admitted, but after months of eating that standard hospital fare, she left the hospital diabetic.

Gradually, I saw the parallels with our broken financial system. Broken money might, in fact, lie at the heart of our broken healthcare system, fostering a high-time-preference model built around medication, billing cycles, and symptom management rather than preventative care and longevity.

I'd always had a strong interest in longevity, but battling chronic pain forced me to dive deeper. Finding answers became essential. Getting out of pain pushed me fully into the longevity rabbit hole.

Doctors rarely discuss nutrition, sleep quality, exercise, or stress management. Medical schools barely touch these areas, even though they are foundational to health. Nutrition education often totals less than 20 hours, while sleep and exercise science are hardly mentioned.

Bitcoin taught me the importance of taking self-custody of my wealth and not blindly trusting the system to have my best interest in mind. I quickly realized the same principle applies to health: If longevity is your goal, you must *take self-custody of your health.*

You have to experiment. You have to question. You have to advocate relentlessly, because the current system isn't designed to guide you toward lifelong health.

Your blood tests and scans might highlight problems, but they seldom reveal underlying causes. Doctors commonly prescribe medications to manage these symptoms without addressing the underlying lifestyle causes. Lasting health improvements lie in daily habits: how you eat, how you move, how you sleep, and how you manage stress, all areas most physicians simply aren't equipped or incentivized to handle.

Your health is, and always has been, in your hands.

A System Built for Sickness

Our healthcare system is built for sickness, not wellness. It excels in emergencies but fails miserably at preventing chronic disease. It might keep you alive, but it won't keep you healthy. Like fiat currency, which inevitably leads to money printing and bailouts, our healthcare is reactive, performing best during crises while steadily deteriorating over time, offering temporary relief instead of long-term solutions.

Walk into a typical clinic with chronic fatigue, anxiety, joint pain, digestive issues, or brain fog, and you're likely to leave with a prescription rather than guidance on diet, sleep, stress, or exercise. Prevention doesn't create repeat customers.

Not to put this on the doctors, either. They operate under tight constraints. They're often overworked, forced into rushed 15-minute appointment windows, with limited resources and training that heavily favors prescribing medication over coaching lifestyle changes. Medical schools provide minimal education on nutrition, sleep, exercise, and stress management, all key elements of long-term health and wellness.

This reactive approach has real-world consequences:

- Over 70% of U.S. adults are overweight or obese.
- Six in ten Americans suffer from at least one preventable chronic disease.

To break free from this reactive model, I realized I needed to start asking myself better questions:

- What am I eating?
- How am I sleeping?

- Am I moving enough?

- Am I chronically stressed or inflamed?

I quickly learned that you can't fix what you don't track and you can't heal what you never examine. Clarity became my most powerful tool, and data became my ally.

Today, I measure nearly everything I can: sleep cycles, glucose levels, inflammation markers, biological age, resting heart rate, heart rate variability, VO_2 max, body fat percentage, visceral fat, and lean body mass. With each measurement, I gain a clearer picture of my health, turning my body into a feedback loop: observe, experiment, adjust, optimize.

Embracing tools like wearables, apps, and AI-powered health platforms transformed my approach. These tools provide insights that the conventional system routinely overlooks. They're empowering, illuminating, and essential for lasting health. In a system that profits from confusion, clarity is your greatest strength.

The Broken Food System

To understand why America's health is failing, look at our plates. Grocery shelves overflow with ultra-processed foods engineered to hit your "bliss point," hijack your dopamine system, and keep you coming back for more.

It's important to note that processed food itself isn't inherently harmful. Processing allows us to preserve, store, and distribute food globally, preventing waste and ensuring year-round access to nutritious food. The harm arises specifically from ultra-processed junk foods, designed primarily for maximum taste and shelf life, typically packed with sugar, salt, artificial flavorings, and empty calories.

More than 75% of U.S. agricultural subsidies go to corn, soy, and wheat, which get processed into cheap oils, syrups, and feed for factory-farmed animals. Meanwhile, nutrient-rich whole foods like fruits and vegetables remain expensive and inconvenient due to deliberate policy decisions rather than free market forces or consumer preferences. Ultimately, this comes down to misaligned incentives.

We've engineered a system where the cheapest and most addictive calories are the most damaging. Chemical-laden produce, hormone-filled meats, and pesticide-soaked grains disrupt your microbiome, causing inflammation and disease.

We're overfed yet undernourished, trapped in a toxic food environment. The evidence is everywhere: rising obesity, diabetes, heart and liver disease, driven by a food system designed to profit from addiction and illness. Severe obesity, defined as having a body mass index (BMI) of 40 or higher, has increased more than sevenfold since 1980 (Figure 10).

Chronic Health Conditions: 1980 vs. 2021-23

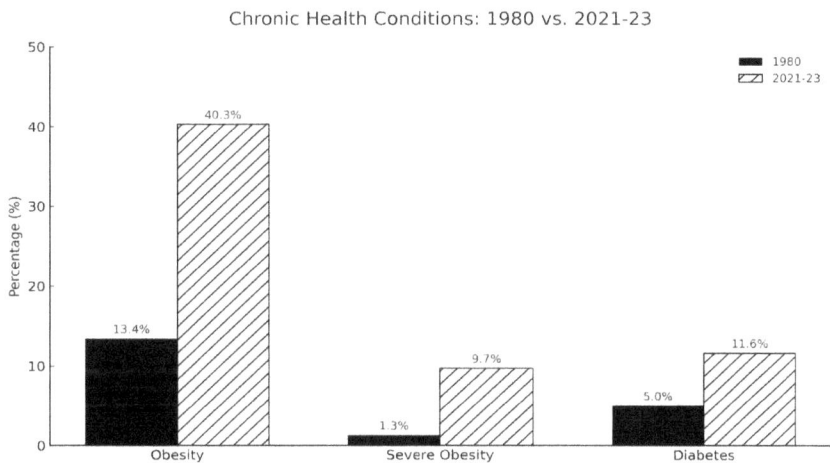

Figure 10: Based on historical and recent CDC data. Chart by Erin E. Malone.

Just as the healthcare system profits from sickness, the food system profits from addiction. The more you eat, the more they profit. The worse you feel, the more you're pushed toward diets, leading to even more ultra-processed, sugary "solutions" appearing in shiny new packages.

This is broken food: mass-produced, heavily marketed, and increasingly disconnected from real nourishment. It's inflation of the worst kind, quietly eroding your health along with your money.

But once you recognize it, you can opt out. Your grocery bill can fund health rather than disease. You can stop feeding the destructive cycle.

Outdated Nutrition Advice

It's not just medical doctors who struggle to guide your long-term health. Dietitians and nutritionists often rely on outdated advice, too. Many still preach calorie counting, low-fat everything, and heavily processed "diet" foods as the keys to health, despite mounting evidence proving otherwise. Recent studies have even linked artificial sweeteners commonly used in these processed "diet" products to increased cancer risk.

I saw this firsthand earlier this year when helping a friend's mom interpret recommendations from her dietitian. The recommendations were outdated and alarming: low-fat yogurt packed with sugar, processed diet drinks filled with artificial sweeteners, highly processed meats, all perfectly acceptable under official guidelines, yet each actively drove chronic inflammation and insulin resistance.

Unfortunately, this scenario isn't unusual:

- **Outdated Guidelines:** Many professionals still refer to dietary recommendations that have remained unchanged for over a decade, ignoring recent research that advocates for healthy fats, low sugar, and minimally processed foods.

- **Biases and Sponsorships:** Studies show nutrition advice often reflects personal biases or industry influence, leading to further confusion and misinformation.

- **Social Media Confusion:** Platforms can amplify outdated advice, reinforcing misconceptions that trap people in harmful dietary patterns.

Just as our healthcare system fails to align with longevity, our nutritional education system is equally broken. It traps people in outdated dietary paradigms that keep chronic illness thriving and the profits flowing.

Like Bitcoin, true sovereignty over your health means questioning conventional wisdom and challenging outdated systems. It requires ongoing education and staying current with evidence-based research.

Remember: you're the best advocate for your health. Stay curious, experiment mindfully, and let clarity and data guide your decisions.

Mining Reward: Stack Polyphenols

Think of polyphenols as the sats of cellular health, small but powerful units that compound over time. Stack them daily with berries, nuts, leafy greens, and extra virgin olive oil. Just like regular bitcoin stacking strengthens your financial health, consistently stacking polyphenols reduces inflammation, boosts immunity, and builds long-term cellular resilience.

Transparency & Third-Party Testing

Another fundamental flaw in our food system is the lack of transparency. When was the last time you knew exactly what was in your food or drinks? Not just from the label, but from independently verified third-party testing? Unfortunately, this type of independent testing is rare, leaving us exposed to hidden contaminants like pesticides, excess sugars, and heavy metals.

Contrast this with pioneering efforts like Bryan Johnson's Blueprint, which openly shares rigorous third-party testing for every ingredient. This transparency sets a powerful precedent, demonstrating what's possible when consumer trust and accountability become core priorities.

Yet companies like Blueprint remain rare exceptions. Fewer than 5% of U.S. food-testing labs meet international accreditation standards, leading to inconsistent and unreliable results. Surveys show a significant gap between consumer desires and market realities: 85% of consumers trust independent third-party certifications, yet only 37% actively look for them. Over 50% of consumers explicitly request clearer and more transparent information about food safety and quality.

Why, then, is transparency still so rare? Why do we tolerate a food system that profits from keeping us in the dark and actively harms our health in the process?

This widespread lack of transparency enables controversial additives to persist. Many ingredients permitted in the U.S. are banned internationally due to significant health risks. While the FDA has finally revoked Red No.

3, artificial colors such as Blue 1, Red 40, and Yellow 5, commonly found in American snacks like Doritos, Skittles, and Gatorade, are prohibited throughout the European Union due to potential adverse health effects. Brominated vegetable oil (BVO), still used in American citrus-flavored beverages, is banned in the EU, Japan, and the U.K. because of neurological and thyroid concerns. Potassium bromate, a dough-strengthening chemical permitted in the U.S., is banned in Europe, China, and India over suspected carcinogenic properties. Even more troubling, azodicarbonamide, a chemical used in American bread and frozen meals to rapidly bleach flour (and also found in yoga mats and sneaker soles), is banned internationally due to its association with respiratory problems.

Glyphosate, the most widely used herbicide in the United States, is another major concern. It is routinely sprayed on genetically modified crops like corn, soy, and wheat, and often ends up in common foods, including cereals and baby formula. The International Agency for Research on Cancer has classified glyphosate as "probably carcinogenic to humans," and many countries, including Germany, France, and Austria, have restricted or banned its use due to growing evidence of health and environmental harm.

True food sovereignty demands ongoing vigilance and active advocacy. Until rigorous transparency becomes standard, you must continually question, investigate, and hold companies accountable. Your health depends on it. Perhaps one day transparency won't be the exception, but the expectation.

Ultra-Processed Foods & Inflammation

Ultra-processed foods are empty calories that carry damaging consequences. Each bite signals your body to store fat, trigger inflammation, disrupt your microbiome, spike blood sugar, and weaken mitochondria.

Packed with refined flours, artificial flavors, emulsifiers, preservatives, and inflammatory industrial seed oils, they systematically degrade your body's health from within. Step into any grocery store, and you're mostly surrounded by industrial chemistry. The long-term health effects of this engineered diet are clear:

- **Chronic low-grade inflammation** is now recognized as a primary driver of heart disease, type 2 diabetes, Alzheimer's, and even depression.

- **Industrial seed oils** such as soybean, corn, and canola, high in pro-inflammatory omega-6 fats, now account for nearly 20% of the average American's daily calorie intake.

- **Overconsumption:** A 2019 NIH study on ultra-processed vs unprocessed food provided participants with carefully matched meals, identical in calories, nutrients, sugar, fat, fiber, and sodium. Participants were allowed to eat as much as they desired. Those on the ultra-processed diet naturally consumed around 500 extra calories per day and gained significant weight, while those eating minimally processed foods ate fewer calories and lost weight.

- **Gut Health Disruption:** Common additives like maltodextrin and carrageenan damage your intestinal lining, worsening conditions like IBS and Crohn's disease.

Calories matter, but metabolic signals matter more. Your body recognizes these additives as threats, triggering immune responses that gradually manifest as brain fog, joint pain, insulin resistance, weight gain, mood swings, and sluggish recovery.

This metabolic self-sabotage is so normalized that we hardly question it. Products labeled as quick meals, low-fat snacks, or energy boosters quietly burn out your cells, often leading you straight into a cycle of prescriptions (Table 5). Food is either fighting for you or against you.

Table 5: Food in the Modern Diet and Health Repercussions

Metric	Statistic
Ultra-processed food share of the U.S. diet	60% of total calories
Daily additive exposure	10 grams of food additives per person
Dementia & inflammation link	Inflammation linked to 91% increased dementia risk
Seed oil consumption increases	1000% rise since 1900
U.S. adult obesity rate	42.4% as of 2020

Data compiled from: Journal of Nutrition (ultra-processed foods), EFSA (daily additives), Neurology (dementia & inflammation), USDA (seed oil consumption), CDC (obesity rate).

Mining Reward: Confirm Your Meals

Think of each meal as a transaction. A short walk afterward helps your body 'confirm' the meal, lowering blood sugar spikes and inflammation. A 10-minute walk locks in metabolic health.

The Business of Sickness

If you want to understand why nothing changes, *follow the money.*

Sickness is big business, and business is booming. A population that's metabolically fit, mentally sharp, and physically strong isn't profitable. Chronic illness is. Statins, insulin, blood pressure medications, antidepressants, and painkillers create lifelong customers, not lasting cures. Even worse, the side effects from these prescriptions are often treated with yet more prescriptions, chasing symptoms rather than addressing underlying causes and compounding the problem.

Consider this: We have more doctors, more prescriptions, and higher healthcare spending than ever before, yet we're sicker, heavier, and dying younger (Figure 11).

Watch network TV for five minutes, and you'll quickly notice the troubling pattern, almost every commercial promotes pharmaceuticals, from pills for cholesterol and diabetes to medications for arthritis, anxiety, and insomnia. Constant medication has become so normalized that we hardly notice the absurdity.

"Big Food" creates metabolic dysfunction, while "Big Pharma" profits by managing the symptoms. Often, these industries share board members, lobbyists, and investors. Companies selling processed snacks and sugary drinks quietly fund diabetes associations and health foundations, effectively disguising strategic marketing as health advocacy. A Cambridge University Press study found that 95% of the 2020–2024 U.S. Dietary Guidelines Advisory Committee had conflicts of interest with major food and pharmaceutical companies, including Kellogg, Abbott, Kraft, Mead Johnson, General Mills, and Dannon.

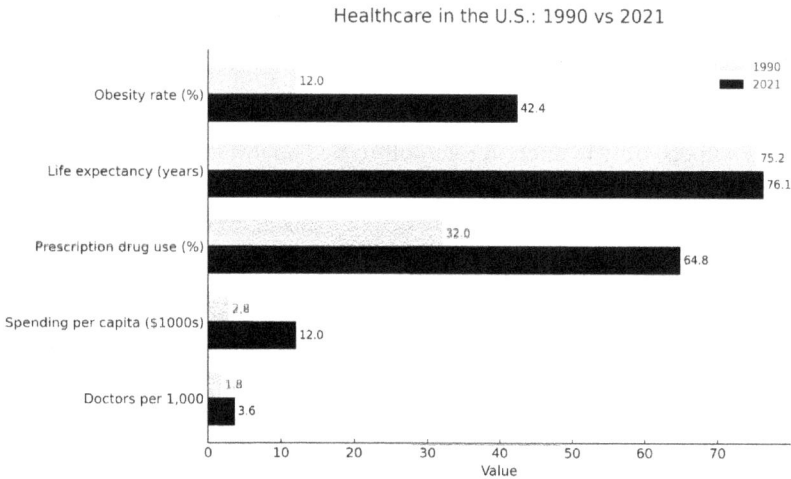

Figure 11: Data compiled from CDC (Obesity, Life Expectancy, Prescription Drug Use), CMS (Healthcare Spending), World Bank (Physicians per 1,000). Chart created by Erin E. Malone.

This distorted incentive structure mirrors exactly what's happening with fiat currency. Both systems reward temporary fixes and short-term thinking, masking deeper problems and slowly fueling long-term decline. You're meant to stay dependent, not to heal.

Even medical research bends to these incentives. Studies that could empower you, like those showing nutrition, sleep, exercise, and fasting can reverse disease, receive minimal funding compared to drugs designed for lifelong dependency.

But there's a way out. Once you recognize these incentives, you can step outside the system. You can become your own investigator, experimenter, and advocate. Understanding how your body truly functions allows you to break free from the cycle.

Taking Control of My Diet

Over a decade ago, I stopped eating meat entirely, including fish, primarily for ethical reasons. To me, the cruelty, environmental harm, and unnecessary killing inherent in factory farming and mass-produced animal agriculture became impossible to justify. As a kid, we had animals as pets:

goats, chickens, ducks, geese, rabbits, and dogs, each with unique personalities and clear intelligence. It always baffled me how we could justify eating some animals but not others. This contradiction became even clearer watching friends raise animals through programs like 4-H, treating them lovingly as pets, only to auction them off to be slaughtered at the year's end. Our modern separation from animal death has always troubled me. I believe this disconnect allows many to justify eating meat. If everyone had to do the killing themselves, we'd likely see many more vegetarians.

I do respect hunters who intentionally select older, weaker, or injured animals nearing the end of their lives. Nature is inherently violent. In the wild, these animals would likely face harsher fates, including starvation, injury, or being hunted by predators, often enduring greater suffering. For me, giving animals a good, full life and responsibly using their meat after a natural or humane death, rather than letting it go to waste, feels ethically justifiable.

Humans no longer need to rely on killing animals to survive. Thanks to advanced agriculture and optimization technologies, we live in a global society capable of growing enough food to sustain everyone year-round. In 2025, approximately 80% of global agricultural land is dedicated to livestock production, including grazing and animal feed, with 40% of all cropland used exclusively to grow feed for animals such as cattle. Yet, only a small sliver of that effort translates into human-edible food: cattle convert just 1-2% of the calories they consume into meat. In other words, for every 100 calories of feed, we get only 1 or 2 calories of beef in return. This stark inefficiency highlights massive waste of land and resources.

In the U.S. alone, over 35% of land area is used solely for grazing, with each cow requiring 10–12 acres per year. Beef production also demands vast amounts of water and emits greenhouse gases, making it a leading contributor to deforestation, biodiversity loss, and pollution. Shifting even a portion of this land to grow crops for direct human consumption would vastly increase food availability, reduce environmental strain, and significantly bolster global food security.

Factory farming intensifies this ethical dilemma even further. Each year, billions of animals endure overcrowded, unsanitary conditions, confined in spaces too cramped for any natural behaviors. To keep them alive and accelerate growth, these animals are routinely given large doses of antibiotics. These antibiotics are used to prevent diseases that inevitably spread in such cruel environments and to artificially boost growth. This widespread antibiotic use has severe consequences, fueling antibiotic-resistant bacteria known as "superbugs." Just in the U.S., antibiotic-resistant infections cause more than 2.8 million illnesses and approximately 35,000 deaths every year. Without meaningful intervention, some estimates project antibiotic resistance could cause as many as 10 million deaths per year globally by 2050.

Factory farming also drives extensive environmental destruction through massive greenhouse gas emissions, water pollution, and habitat loss. Animal agriculture alone accounts for roughly 14.5% of global greenhouse gas emissions. Runoff from concentrated animal feeding operations (CAFOs) pollutes waterways and contaminates surrounding communities with methane, ammonia, pathogens, and antibiotic-resistant bacteria.

Ultimately, factory farming is a system built on cruelty, fundamentally disconnected from nature, and driven primarily by efficiency and profit, with little regard for animal welfare, environmental sustainability, or human health.

Recognizing these ethical and environmental challenges prompted deeper reflection about my own diet and health. I began to look more critically at what I was eating, questioning habits I'd never considered before.

While struggling with digestive issues in my early 20s, an elimination diet revealed I was dairy intolerant, prompting me to gradually cut dairy from my diet. Dairy intolerance is surprisingly common, affecting about 75% of people worldwide, often without them even knowing it. This process opened my eyes to how frequently dairy sneaks into a wide variety of foods.

A couple of years later, when I shifted to a 100% plant-based diet, the benefits quickly became clear. Food comas disappeared, and I no longer felt sluggish or needed naps after eating. My digestive system stabilized, energy levels rose dramatically, and combined with regular exercise, I became stronger than ever. About a year ago, I even accomplished my first-ever pull-up, something I couldn't do even as a kid.

While plant-based eating has substantial benefits, it can be challenging compared to simpler diets like carnivore, where meal choices are straightforward. On a plant-based diet, it's easy to slip into ultra-processed convenience foods lacking nutrients. To succeed, structure and planning are critical. Meal prepping is essential. I usually prepare meals several days in advance, especially during busy weeks. I regularly seek out new recipes to keep meals fresh, interesting, and nutritious To minimize plastic, I use stainless steel containers, which also help control portion sizes. Currently, my go-to meal prep containers are from Black+Blum (they're even microwave-safe).

Staples in my diet include:

- Vegetables: Broccoli, cauliflower, squash, mushrooms, kale, peppers, eggplant, cabbage, tomatoes, sweet potatoes, carrots. I prioritize local, organic produce with a lot of vibrant colors.

- Fruits: Berries, bananas, avocados, apples.

- Grains & legumes: Quinoa, lentils, beans, brown or wild rice, chickpeas, chickpea pasta.

- Dairy alternatives: Unsweetened coconut or cashew yogurt, low-sugar oat milk.

- Snacks & extras: Low-sugar granola, popcorn, nutritional yeast (high in B12, tastes like parmesan), dark chocolate (ideally tested for heavy metals and contaminants)

- Nuts & seeds: Pistachios, macadamias, cashews, walnuts, hemp seeds, flaxseed.

- Protein sources: Tofu, tempeh, quinoa, lentils, beans, chickpeas, and protein powders (Blueprint Longevity, Vega).

- Drinks: Coffee, matcha, Blueprint Longevity mix.

- Extra Virgin Olive Oil drizzled on meals (preferably single-source, high in polyphenols).

- Organic Coconut Oil for cooking

Facing My Genetic Risks

A few years ago, I decided to take a genetic test. The results shook me awake. Turns out I carry two copies of the APOE ε4 gene, which significantly increases my risk for Alzheimer's disease by about 10 to 15 times compared to the general population. By the time I'm 85, there's nearly a 60% chance I'll develop Alzheimer's dementia.

Discovering this felt like uncovering a hidden time bomb that had been quietly ticking inside me. Those abstract statistics suddenly became deeply personal, urgent, and real. It kicked me into an entirely new gear. Waiting passively for symptoms to emerge wasn't an option; I had to act immediately.

Almost overnight, I radically transformed my lifestyle. I'd already been eating a plant-based diet for eight years, supported by research linking such diets to reduced dementia risks. But now, I doubled down. I aggressively cut inflammatory foods, dramatically reduced sugar, and reserved alcohol for rare occasions. Intermittent fasting became routine to boost insulin sensitivity and metabolic health, both crucial for cognitive longevity.

Regular cardiovascular exercise also became non-negotiable for maintaining healthy circulation and cognitive resilience. Protecting my brain became just as important as protecting my body. Discovering my genetic risks motivated me to actively seek new, mentally engaging experiences like rock climbing and specifically bouldering, which demands intense physical precision, problem-solving, and mental focus. I earned my personal trainer certification, diving deeper into exercise science and its connection to cognitive health. Regular engagement with complex skills keeps my brain adaptable and resilient.

We live in an unprecedented moment in history. With rapid advancements in AI, abundant access to data, and increasingly precise and affordable bloodwork and genetic testing, health insights that were once inaccessible or prohibitively expensive are now within our reach. By embracing these powerful tools, we can proactively identify risks, optimize our health, and significantly delay or even prevent many diseases previously considered inevitable.

My story isn't unique. Millions carry hidden genetic risks, silent threats waiting beneath the surface. But you can't change what you don't know. Everyone should know their genetic data. Data isn't something to fear; it's your strongest ally. Test proactively. Experiment intentionally.

You can't experience the future you're building if you're not here to see it. Future-proofing your life means facing your risks head-on and taking intentional steps today to remain healthy, vibrant, and prepared for the opportunities ahead. With rapid advancements and breakthroughs emerging daily, the future is thrilling yet impossible to fully grasp. We're on the brink of creating superintelligence, and we may even solve aging itself.

Discovering my genetic risk made it crystal clear: if you're not proactively testing and tracking your health, you risk falling through the cracks. How many people have died because simple genetic screenings or proactive tests weren't standard practice? Our healthcare system isn't built to prevent disease or optimize long-term health. It's built around managing symptoms after they appear. Stepping outside this system begins with realizing no one cares about your health as much as you do. No one's coming to save you. The good news? You don't need them to. All you need are the right tools, accurate data, and the willingness to take action.

Supplements and Targeted Strategies

Doctors often worry that plant-based diets lack certain nutrients, particularly vitamin B12, but nutritional yeast and tempeh effectively cover my B12 needs. My latest blood tests placed my B12 levels in the optimal range. I aim to get a comprehensive, 100+ biomarker blood panel every six months (see Mining Reward: Get a Full Blood Panel).

Regular blood testing helps identify and address nutritional gaps. Vitamin D deficiency is widespread, significantly affecting immune health and outcomes from illnesses, including COVID-19. Several studies have found that a large percentage of people severely affected by COVID-19 were deficient in vitamin D. This deficiency was linked to significantly worse outcomes, including up to an 80% higher risk of hospitalization or death. If you decide to supplement Vitamin D, it's recommended to pair it with Vitamin K2 to enhance absorption.

Because brain health is a major priority for me, especially given my genetic risks, I pay careful attention to specific supplements. Omega-3s and creatine are among the safest and most extensively studied supplements for cognitive and overall health. I personally use a high-quality vegan omega-3 supplement (algae-based), aiming for 1,500–2,000 mg daily, specifically targeting EPA (1,000–1,500 mg) and DHA (500–1,000 mg). My daily creatine intake is around 5 grams. Creatine may not be suitable for people with kidney issues, so always test and understand your personal health markers first. I also supplement a few times a week with Magnesium L-threonate (about 2,000 mg per session, providing around 144 mg of elemental magnesium), known for cognitive and memory benefits. A good starting dose for omega-3 is typically 1,000–2,000 mg per day, while creatine supplementation usually begins around 3–5 grams per day. When it comes to supplements, always do your own research, regularly test for deficiencies, and analyze your results with AI health platforms. Every individual is unique, and supplementation and diet should be personalized accordingly.

Another critical strategy is time-restricted eating. My daily eating window is around eight hours. I typically stick to 7:30 am–3:30 pm, with a firm cutoff at 4 pm. This prevents overeating and late-night snacking, profoundly improving my sleep, which we'll discuss further in the next chapter. When I first adopted this schedule, I shed over 10% of my body fat in just three months, and 15% in six months. Life sometimes interferes, so it's important to find an eating window that suits your lifestyle. I'm usually hungriest in the morning, while others might prefer skipping breakfast. Ultimately, restricting your eating window helps control calorie intake and reduce overeating.

Microbiome testing is another tool worth exploring. Tests vary in accuracy. Some rely on a single sample, while others test repeatedly over weeks. However, since your microbiome naturally shifts about every six months, the long-term usefulness of these tests can be questionable. Often, experimenting through dietary elimination and reintroduction provides clearer personal insights, as it did for me with dairy intolerance.

Ultimately, using data and experimentation to pinpoint exactly what your body needs is key. Regularly adjust your food choices and supplementation based on results, retesting periodically.

Test, experiment based on your data, then test again.

Mining Reward: Get a Full Blood Panel

Most standard checkups miss the big picture. Doctors rarely order more than a few surface-level tests. If you want real insight into your health, order a comprehensive blood panel. You can test over 100 biomarkers, including hormones, inflammation, nutrientlevels, and metabolic function, for a few hundred dollars as of 2025.

Getting a baseline gives you something solid to work with. It's the foundation for making smart, targeted decisions that actually move you forward. These panels are available through providers such as Labcorp, Quest Diagnostics, or services like Function Health. I personally ordered mine through Blueprint. com, which uses Labcorp for collection. Afterward, I imported the results into the Don't Die app, which translated the raw data into clear, actionable insights. You can also use AI tools or other health platforms to interpret your results and guide you toward personalized next steps.

Blue Zones and the Power of Plant-Based Eating

The dietary principles of Blue Zones (regions with notably high concentrations of centenarians) align closely with both my personal health experience and my research into longevity. Across these diverse communities, a predominantly plant-based diet is common. In Okinawa, Japan, nearly 90% of their traditional diet consists of whole plant foods such as sweet potatoes, vegetables, legumes, and rice. Okinawans consume about 80% fewer dairy products and meat compared to average Western diets, contributing to exceptionally low rates of cardiovascular disease and cancers.

Another key practice in Okinawa is called **hara hachi bu**, or eating until you're about 80% full. Unlike in the U.S., where portion sizes have grown dramatically over the decades, Okinawans consciously moderate portions and eat slowly. This mindful eating practice naturally leads to lower calorie consumption and supports long-term metabolic health. Their traditional foods, such as nutrient-dense tofu, vegetables, and sweet potatoes, are filling yet lower in calories and rich in dietary fiber. Okinawans can consume larger volumes of food, feeling comfortably satisfied without overeating.

In Costa Rica's Nicoya Peninsula, beans, corn, and squash form the cornerstone of daily eating, providing high amounts of dietary fiber, often over 25 grams per day, which research consistently links to a lower risk of heart disease, stroke, and diabetes. Similarly, residents in Sardinia, Italy, rely heavily on whole grains, legumes, fresh vegetables, fruits, nuts, and olive oil. Studies of Sardinian centenarians show significantly lower blood pressure, cholesterol, and inflammation levels compared to their Western counterparts, directly correlating with their dietary patterns.

Overall, populations in these Blue Zones experience dramatically lower rates of chronic illnesses. For example, the Adventist Health Study, conducted in Loma Linda, California, found that individuals who ate a plant-based diet had approximately a 30% lower risk of cardiovascular disease and a 15% lower risk of all-cause mortality compared to those who regularly consumed meat. Dementia rates across all Blue Zones are also substantially lower than global averages, reflecting their diets rich in vegetables, fruits, legumes, and healthy fats, as well as their active lifestyles and strong social connections. Ikaria, Greece, is particularly extraordinary, with dementia cases nearly non-existent.

These plant-rich diets, rich in antioxidants, fiber, and polyphenols, help support a strong immune system, promote healthier digestion, reduce inflammation, and enhance cognitive function… all critical pieces of staying sharp, healthy, and independent as you age. But remember, your health data and individual responses are key. Keep testing, experimenting, and adjusting based on what works best for your body.

Importantly, thriving on a plant-centered diet doesn't necessarily require strict veganism or vegetarianism; many Blue Zone communities still include modest amounts of animal products. However, the common denominator is clear: plants overwhelmingly form the dietary foundation, often comprising 80–95% of total daily calories.

While the dietary insights from Blue Zones strongly support my personal choices, I also know there's no one-size-fits-all approach to nutrition. What works perfectly for one person may not be ideal for another. Ultimately, the most effective strategy is to gather your own health data, experiment thoughtfully, and adjust your diet based on what your body responds to best.

Escaping the System

For most people, survival comes first. Health falls somewhere further down the list. They're stuck running endlessly on a hamster wheel, working multiple jobs, juggling constant demands, and barely keeping up while their time and energy erode under broken financial incentives. It's no wonder convenience wins over nourishment. When every minute of your day is spent just trying to stay afloat, prioritizing real health can feel like an impossible luxury.

I remember this feeling of desperation vividly. It defined so much of my life and is deeply engrained in who I am. In high school, I worked at my town's only grocery store, grabbing day-old donuts or cheap hot dogs during short breaks, not because I didn't want healthier choices, but because those calories were all I could afford. Our school hallways were lined with vending machines selling nothing but Mountain Dew and candy bars. Breakfast meant Pop-Tarts, and lunch was a reheated tray of processed mystery food. From childhood, we're subtly conditioned to accept this diet of ultra-processed sugar and artificial ingredients as entirely normal. When you're down to counting quarters, fresh produce isn't even on your radar. Cheap calories become survival food. But surviving is not thriving.

Inflation quietly steals our purchasing power, pushing basic nutrition further out of reach (Table 6). In countries experiencing hyperinflation, entire life savings evaporate overnight, plunging people into perpetual survival mode. Even in the U.S., inflation silently erodes our time each day. Money saved today buys less tomorrow. When your time is continuously devalued, self-care, sleep, exercise, and mindful eating quickly become unaffordable luxuries.

Let's look at the numbers:

Table 6: Inflation Rate and the Loss of Purchasing Power

Inflation Rate	Years to 50% Loss in Purchasing Power
2%	36 Years
4%	18 Years
12%	6 Years
24%	2 Years

At just 2% inflation, your savings lose half their purchasing power in 36 years. At 4%, it takes only 18 years. At higher rates, such as those recently experienced globally, your money and time evaporate even faster.

These numbers profoundly affect people's lives. Inflation is like holding a melting ice cube in your hand, slowly dripping away your savings. It forces you to run faster, work longer, and continually sacrifice your health.

The solution begins by fixing money itself.

Bitcoin represents sound money, something fundamentally stronger than just another investment. Secure, verifiable, and scarce, bitcoin preserves your time and energy. Instead of watching your savings quietly erode, bitcoin protects the hours you've worked, the effort you've invested, and the life you've exchanged.

With sound money, your time becomes yours again. You no longer have to sprint just to stand still. Instead, you regain the capacity to invest in real health: nutritious food, restful sleep, intentional movement, and personal sovereignty.

The connection is clear. Fix your money, and you can fix your life.

When incentives align around truth, longevity, and proof of work, genuine health becomes attainable. You step off the hamster wheel of survival mode and into true empowerment. You finally have the space and stability to build strong foundations, whether vibrant health, sustainable wealth, or simply a life that improves every year.

That's how you escape the system and future-proof your life.

Recipe: Anti-Inflammatory Longevity Bowl

Serves: 2

This vibrant, plant-based bowl actively fights inflammation, balances your blood sugar, and deeply nourishes your body, serving as the nutritional antidote to ultra-processed fiat foods. Each ingredient supports your journey to reclaim health sovereignty and future-proof your life.

Ingredients:

- Base:
    - 1 cup quinoa (rich in protein, fiber, antioxidants)
    - 1 cup fresh kale or spinach (high in antioxidants, iron, vitamins)
- Veggie Toppings:
    - ½ avocado, sliced (healthy fats, potassium)
    - 1 medium sweet potato, peeled and cubed (high in fiber, beta-ca-ro-tene)
    - 1 cup broccoli florets (sulforaphane-rich, anti-cancer properties)
    - ½ cup purple cabbage, thinly sliced (rich in antioxidants, supports gut health)
- Plant-based Protein:
    - 4 oz tempeh or ¾ cup seasoned chickpeas (protein-rich, high fiber)
- Anti-Inflammatory Dressing:
    - 2 tbsp extra-virgin olive oil
    - 1 tbsp fresh lemon juice
    - ½ tsp turmeric powder
    - ¼ tsp black pepper (enhances turmeric absorption)
    - 1 tsp freshly grated ginger
    - Pinch of sea salt

Instructions:

1. Cook the quinoa according to the package instructions; let it cool slightly.

2. Roast sweet potato cubes and broccoli at 400°F for 20–25 minutes until tender and lightly browned.

3. Sauté tempeh or chickpeas in a pan with olive oil, salt, pepper, and your choice of spices (e.g., smoked paprika or cumin) until golden.

4. Prepare dressing by whisking olive oil, lemon juice, turmeric, ginger, black pepper, and sea salt until well combined.

5. Assemble bowl: layer quinoa at the base, add leafy greens, roasted veggies, avocado slices, and protein.

6. Generously drizzle with the anti-inflammatory dressing.

Why this works:

- Turmeric, ginger, and extra-virgin olive oil have been shown to actively reduce inflammation and oxidative stress.

- Healthy fats from avocado and olive oil support cellular function and hormone balance.

- High fiber ingredients stabilize blood sugar and support gut health, naturally reducing inflammation.

Bio Age Testing Recipe

The following benchmarks represent *average healthy ranges* based on current scientific understanding. Remember that everyone's baseline differs, and new research continually refines these targets. Use this table as a practical guide, not absolute law, to measure your progress and optimize your health over time (Table 7).

Table 7: Average Healthy Ranges of Fitness Standards

Metric	Age	Men	Women
Grip Strength (lbs)	20–29 yrs	≥101 lbs	≥62 lbs
	30–39 yrs	≥97 lbs	≥57 lbs
	40–49 yrs	≥92 lbs	≥53 lbs
	50–59 yrs	≥88 lbs	≥49 lbs
	60+ yrs	≥79 lbs	≥44 lbs
Push-Up Test	20–29 yrs	≥30 reps	≥20 reps
	30–39 yrs	≥25 reps	≥15 reps
	40–49 yrs	≥20 reps	≥12 reps
	50–59 yrs	≥15 reps	≥8 reps
	60+ yrs	≥10 reps	≥5 reps
Plank Hold (sec)	20–39 yrs	≥90 sec	≥90 sec
	40–59 yrs	≥75 sec	≥75 sec
	60+ yrs	≥60 sec	≥60 sec
One-Leg Balance (sec)	20–39 yrs	≥60 sec	≥60 sec
	40–59 yrs	≥45 sec	≥45 sec
	60+ yrs	≥30 sec	≥30 sec
Dead Hang (sec)	20–39 yrs	≥60 sec	≥45 sec
	40–59 yrs	≥45 sec	≥30 sec
	60+ yrs	≥30 sec	≥20 sec
Sit-and-Reach (inches)	20–39 yrs	0–2 in	2–4 in
	40–59 yrs	≥0 in	1–3 in
	60+ yrs	≥-2 in	0–2 in
Sit-to-Stand (reps)	20–39 yrs	≥15 reps	≥15 reps

Metric	Age	Men	Women
	40–59 yrs	≥12 reps	≥12 reps

Compiled from American College of Sports Medicine (ACSM) guidelines, National Strength and Conditioning Association (NSCA) standards. CDC Physical Activity Guidelines, and National Institutes of Health (NIH) Physical Fitness Assessment Data. Created by Erin E. Malone.

How to Use This Table:

- Find your age range and gender.

- Compare your results with these benchmarks.

- Track your progress regularly, aiming for incremental improvements over time.

- Use these benchmarks as guidelines, not strict rules. Your primary goal is consistent improvement through mindful experimentation. As new research emerges, our understanding of optimal health will evolve as well.

- To measure grip strength, you can purchase a grip strength dynamometer (available online for around $25).

- For One-Leg Balance, stand upright on one foot without holding onto anything or using external support, and time how long you can maintain your balance before placing your raised foot down or needing support.

- For Dead Hang, grip an overhead bar firmly and lift your feet off the ground, hanging freely without swinging or pulling yourself upward. Time how long you can maintain your grip until your hands slip or you need to release the bar.

- For Sit-and-Reach, sit with your legs fully extended in front of you, you reach forward as far as possible toward (or past) your toes. The measurement indicates how close you can get to or how far past your toes you can reach, in inches. Positive numbers indicate reaching past your toes, while negative numbers indicate you're short of reaching your toes.

- For Sit-to-Stand, sit in a sturdy chair and count how many times you can stand fully upright and then sit back down within 30 seconds.

Chapter 6

Layered Systems: Sleep as Layer 1

When I was a kid, we had this scary old two-story barn on our property. It was well over a hundred years old, with broken-out windows and weathered, peeling paint. On windy days, I remember hearing the eerie, howling sound as air whistled through the shattered panes and loose boards. Shreds of old cloth flapped around inside like ghosts, caught in perpetual motion. Inside, the floorboards had rotted away, leaving gaping holes that exposed the dark earth below. I distinctly remember staring down through those openings, fixated on the dirt beneath my feet, feeling my heart race as I carefully stepped around each weakened board. Ancient tools lay half-buried nearby, caked in decades' worth of dust and draped in thick, spiderwebbed layers, like relics from another era.

Despite the crumbling base, the walls and upper level still looked surprisingly intact. My brother and I were repeatedly warned not to go anywhere near it. My parents insisted the barn was unsafe and could collapse at any moment. I was only inside once or twice with my parents, probably before it had fully deteriorated. Still, I vividly remember the fear I felt, sensing the danger lurking beneath me with every cautious step.

Then one morning, when I was about six years old, I woke up, looked outside, and saw the barn had completely collapsed. Overnight, its rotting foundation had finally given way, bringing down everything that had seemed solid above.

Secure Your Base Layer First

Your health functions exactly like that barn. No matter how impressive your upper layers might look, advanced training routines, supplements, precision nutrition plans, or **biohacking** strategies, they're useless without a secure, well-maintained foundation. If the base is neglected, everything built on top inevitably collapses.

You can't future-proof your life without securing the fundamentals: sleep, hydration, and basic nutrition. These elements form your body's *base layer*, the essential foundation upon which your overall health and resilience depend.

In Bitcoin terms, **the base layer** (also known as **Layer 1**) is the fundamental network that securely processes, verifies, and permanently records all transactions. Think of Bitcoin's Layer 1 as an ultra-secure digital vault, providing an unshakeable foundation for every transaction and network activity built upon it. Without this stable and secure base, Bitcoin's upper layers, like Lightning, financial applications, and exchanges, would collapse. Similarly, the internet relies entirely on its foundational base protocol, TCP/IP. Without TCP/IP, our digital infrastructure (banks, stock markets, online payments, websites, apps) would crumble.

Your health operates in exactly the same way. Quality sleep, proper hydration, and essential nutrition form your biological Layer 1, the irreplaceable foundation for metabolic health, hormonal balance, fitness performance, memory, and emotional stability. If your biological base layer weakens, everything built on top inevitably crumbles. Of these essentials, sleep stands out. It isn't just passive rest; it's a critical, restorative process fundamental for peak performance, sustained health, and lasting well-being. Yet most people today treat sleep as an inconvenience, rarely giving it the care or respect it truly deserves.

The Layered System: Bitcoin and Beyond

Bitcoin's foundational Layer 1 ensures security, decentralization, and immutability. To globally scale Bitcoin and enable fast, low-cost transactions, second-layer solutions were developed. While several Layer 2 protocols exist, the Lightning Network is uniquely permissionless and built directly upon Bitcoin itself, eliminating the need for third-party trust or counterparty risk.

Lightning leverages Bitcoin's robust security and open network to facilitate instant, nearly free transactions accessible worldwide. Traditional international money transfers remain slow, expensive, and complicated. Sending money from the U.S. to Mexico through services like Western Union can cost up to $45 and take days, often leaving recipients significantly short-changed. Even domestically, bank-to-bank transfers frequently take multiple days to settle and often involve fees. Businesses typically lose around 3% on credit card transactions and may have to wait a month for funds to fully clear.

Bitcoin's Lightning Network solves these problems. Payments settle instantly with minimal fees, often fractions of a cent. Businesses dramatically reduce transaction costs and gain immediate access to funds. Companies like Strike use Lightning to instantly convert dollars into pesos across borders, entirely bypassing traditional delays and excessive fees. Lightning offers a scalable, practical solution tailored precisely for today's global economic needs: instant, borderless, and affordable transactions accessible to everyone.

Above Lightning, Layer 3 solutions and integrations like **Nostr**, Cashu, Fedimint, Zeus, Strike, and various exchanges simplify everyday inter-actions with Bitcoin. Yet all these higher-level tools depend entirely on Bitcoin's foundational Layer 1. Similarly, your advanced health practices rely completely on strong foundational habits: quality sleep, nutrition, and hydration.

Mining Reward: Instant Global Value Transfer

Stop losing money to international transfer fees and delays. Use the Lightning Network to instantly send and receive funds worldwide for fractions of a cent. Move value seamlessly, bypass traditional financial roadblocks, and reclaim your money and time.

Make Sleep Non-Negotiable

Health optimization works a lot like Bitcoin's layered system: it doesn't matter how advanced your upper layers become if your foundation isn't solid. For me, that foundational Layer 1 starts with sleep, along with proper hydration and basic nutrition, with sleep always being my highest priority.

I learned the hard way that sleep is non-negotiable. I spent years experimenting with specialized diets, intense training programs, biohacking, and various cognitive routines, always searching for that extra edge. But none of these advanced practices truly moved the needle until I fixed my sleep. Eventually, I realized I could eat perfectly, train consistently, and cultivate excellent habits, but without high-quality, restorative sleep, my body and mind inevitably broke down.

Even one poor night's sleep noticeably impacts my mental clarity, mood, and physical recovery. After a few days of compromised sleep, I can literally feel my health declining: my resting heart rate rises, my workouts become sluggish, and my mental sharpness fades.

Through obsessive tracking, I've repeatedly seen just how critical sleep is. Now, sleep is always my first priority. Once I secured sleep as my base layer, every other health practice started delivering far better results.

Sleep Deprivation: The Invisible Damage

Recent studies highlight the serious cognitive consequences of sleep deprivation:

- One night of total sleep deprivation increases beta-amyloid in the brain by 5%, the same plaque associated with Alzheimer's disease.

- Sleep loss raises S100-B and NSE biomarkers by 20%, markers typically observed following traumatic brain injury and stroke.

- Sleep deprivation significantly impairs attention, working memory, and decision-making skills, with effects comparable to mild brain trauma.

- Chronic sleep loss lowers IQ, impairs executive function, increases anxiety, and accelerates cellular aging.

In *Why We Sleep*, Dr. Matthew Walker outlines how sleep deprivation mimics cognitive decline, weakens the immune system, and distorts emotional regulation. After more than 20 years studying sleep, Walker, a professor at UC Berkeley, describes sleep as "the single most effective thing you can do to reset your brain and body health." His research demonstrates that a lack of sleep:

- Lowers immune function by up to 70%.

- Reduces learning capacity by about 40%.

- Significantly increases the risk for cancer, cardiovascular disease, and Alzheimer's.

- Shortens lifespan.

Evolution's Sleep Paradox

From an evolutionary perspective, sleep seems counterintuitive. We spend nearly one-third of our lives unconscious, a considerable survival risk for prehistoric humans surrounded by constant threats. If evolution could have eliminated sleep, natural selection would have favored those needing less of it. Yet, despite millions of years of intense evolutionary pressure, sleep persists universally across nearly every species on Earth because its restorative benefits far outweigh these risks.

Key restorative functions of sleep include:

- **Brain Detoxification:** activating the **glymphatic system**, a unique waste clearance pathway that flushes out harmful toxins and metabolic waste products, such as beta-amyloid, a protein fragment whose buildup forms plaques closely linked to Alzheimer's disease.

- **Immune System Recalibration:** actively redistributing immune cells throughout the body, significantly reducing inflammation, enhancing tissue repair, and strengthening your defense against illness and infections.

- **Hormonal and Metabolic Regulation:** precisely regulating hormones that control metabolism, appetite, stress response, and mood, which significantly reduces the risk of obesity, diabetes, cardiovascular diseases, and mood disorders.

- **Memory and Emotional Processing:** actively reorganizing and consolidating memories, strengthening neural pathways critical for learning, and improving emotional regulation and resilience, making you better equipped to manage stress and maintain mental clarity.

Evolution retained sleep because chronic sleep deprivation severely compromises survival and overall health. Sleep is the most foundational investment you can make in your biological future.

Optimizing Your Sleep Protocol

To optimize your sleep, consider implementing the following strategies:

- **Consistent Sleep Schedule**: Aim for 7–9 hours of sleep per night, consistently going to bed and waking up at the same times daily to regulate your circadian rhythm.

- **Pre-Sleep Routine**: Before bed, engage in calming activities such as reading or meditation to signal your body that it's time to wind down.

- **Environment**: Ensure your bedroom is cool, dark, and quiet. If necessary, consider using blackout curtains and white noise machines.

- **Limit Stimulants**: Avoid caffeine and electronic screens in the hours leading up to bedtime, as they can interfere with your body's natural sleep signals.

- **Nutrition**: Finish eating at least 2–3 hours before bed to allow your body to focus on restorative processes rather than digestion. If you must eat closer to bedtime, try to keep it light.

Heart Rate, HRV, and Sleep Quality

Your body communicates every night; you just need to know how to listen. Two key indicators of your sleep quality and overall health are resting heart rate (RHR) and heart rate variability (HRV).

Resting Heart Rate (RHR) is the number of times your heart beats per minute when you're completely at rest. Generally, a lower RHR is associated with better cardiovascular fitness and lower stress levels.

Heart Rate Variability (HRV) measures the slight variations between your heartbeats. Generally, a higher HRV indicates that your body is effectively shifting into its parasympathetic state, the "rest and digest" mode crucial for recovery and stress reduction.

When I first started tracking my sleep, clear patterns quickly emerged. Late dinners, heavy meals eaten close to bedtime, or working late into the evening noticeably elevated my RHR and kept it elevated throughout the night, resulting in fragmented sleep with noticeably less deep sleep. Earlier meal timing significantly lowered my RHR, increased my HRV, and enhanced my deep sleep quality. Intense late-evening workouts or lingering stress often raised my RHR and decreased my HRV, negatively affecting sleep. Even moderate alcohol consumption, like a single glass of wine, measurably increased my RHR, reduced HRV, and disrupted my overall sleep quality.

These numbers directly reflected how I felt the next day: groggy, unfocused, and sluggish. An elevated RHR at bedtime clearly indicated that my body was still processing stress, alcohol, or late meals, hindering its ability to fully enter recovery mode.

Research confirms these experiences. A recent study in *Sleep Medicine Reviews* demonstrated that for every 10-beat-per-minute increase in nighttime RHR, sleep quality significantly declines. On nights when I finished dinner at least four hours before bed, my RHR noticeably dropped, sleep came more easily, and I woke up feeling sharper. My sleep tracking data consistently showed longer stretches of uninterrupted deep sleep on these nights, correlating directly with better mental clarity and physical performance the next day.

My HRV values consistently supported these observations. During stressful periods, such as approaching deadlines, disrupted routines due to travel, or heightened emotional strain, my HRV dropped dramatically, locking my body into survival mode, preventing deep, restorative sleep. In 2023, the American Heart Association confirmed that higher nighttime HRV correlates with improved cognitive performance, reduced inflammation, and lower cardiovascular risk. Clearly, HRV can offer essential insights into your body's internal balance between stress and recovery.

Interestingly, my husband experiences similar yet distinct patterns. While meal timing influences his sleep, the quality and amount of food he consumes matter even more. On days when he doesn't eat enough or chooses lower-quality food, his sleep suffers noticeably, regardless of timing. Studies back this up, showing inadequate caloric intake or poor dietary choices elevate stress hormones such as cortisol and adrenaline, disrupting sleep depth and continuity.

This highlights just how personal sleep optimization truly is. Meal timing significantly impacts my sleep, whereas food quantity and quality affect my husband more. Yet for both of us, food quality matters significantly: nutrient-dense, anti-inflammatory foods consistently lead to better sleep metrics. The key takeaway? Pay attention, track your data, and experiment to discover what actually works for your body. Everyone is different; identifying your optimal sleep protocol is crucial for long-term health.

It's fascinating to see how consistently RHR and HRV move in opposite directions. On nights when I'm relaxed and maintaining good habits, my RHR drops and HRV rises, clearly showing my body is in balance and recovery mode. However, when stress or unhealthy habits enter the picture, the opposite happens: my resting heart rate increases, my HRV decreases, and my sleep suffers, with noticeably reduced deep sleep, fragmented REM cycles, and noticeably compromised recovery.

Through careful tracking, I've learned to interpret my body's subtle signals and adjust accordingly. I use an Apple Watch for tracking, but any wearable device can provide valuable insights (Oura Ring, Fitbit, and Whoop, etc.). Adjusting meal timing, prioritizing nutrient-rich foods, creating calming evening routines, incorporating meditation or breathwork, and even optimizing bedroom temperature each directly improve these metrics and enhance my sleep quality.

Learning to optimize my RHR and HRV transformed my approach to sleep. Instead of guessing if I'm rested, now I know. I understand exactly which behaviors support my body's foundational recovery processes, and I have the data to prove it.

Sleep Stages

You don't just need more sleep, you need the right kinds. Sleep involves distinct phases, each playing a crucial role in your health and performance. Many people spend eight, nine, or even ten hours in bed, yet still wake up feeling exhausted because they unknowingly miss out on sufficient deep or REM sleep. Tracking these sleep phases can reveal if your sleep is truly restorative or just time spent lying in bed.

During **deep sleep,** your brain activates the glymphatic system to clear out toxins and metabolic waste. This phase also solidifies short-term memories into long-term storage and supports physical recovery by releasing growth hormones essential for muscle and tissue repair.

REM (Rapid Eye Movement) sleep serves a different but equally important role. This stage processes emotions, integrates daily experiences, enhances creativity, and supports skill-based memory, helping you master movements, tasks, and problem-solving skills.

Both deep sleep and REM naturally diminish with age, stress, alcohol consumption, and irregular sleep patterns. During a typical night, we cycle repeatedly through these four distinct stages:

• **Light Sleep** (NREM stages 1 and 2): Transition stages that begin memory processing.

• **Deep Sleep** (NREM stage 3): Predominates early in the night, crucial for physical and neurological recovery.

• **REM Sleep:** Short initially but lengthens towards morning, essential for cognitive function and emotional health

Most consumer wearables simplify these stages into just three categories: REM, light, and deep, combining NREM stages 1 and 2 into one light sleep category often called "core sleep." My Apple Watch data (Figure 12) consistently confirms research findings, showing deep sleep mostly occurs earlier in the night, while REM sleep increases toward morning.

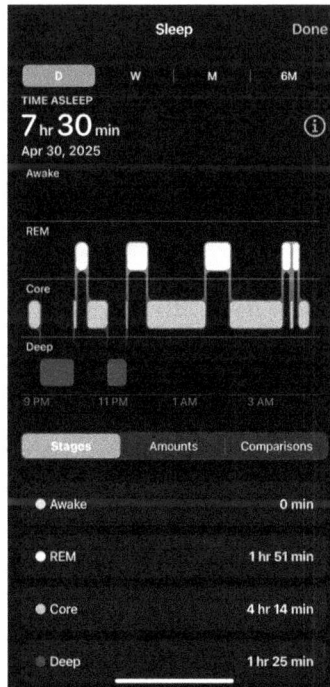

Figure 12: Sleep data from an Apple Watch.

117

Circadian Rhythm, Melatonin, and Light Exposure

Your body follows a natural internal clock called the **circadian rhythm**, which cycles roughly every 24 hours. This rhythm explains why you might naturally wake up right before your alarm and feel sleepy around the same time each night. Shortly after waking, your sleep drive is at its lowest, gradually building throughout the day until reaching its peak around your usual bedtime. Similarly, your core body temperature aligns with this cycle, rising to its highest in the late afternoon or early evening, coinciding with peak physical performance, coordination, and cognitive sharpness (interestingly, this is also when most Olympic records are set). Overnight, your core temperature drops to its lowest point, enabling deep and restorative sleep.

Central to your circadian rhythm is melatonin, a hormone produced by the pineal gland in your brain. Melatonin levels naturally rise in darkness, signaling it's time for sleep, and fall with exposure to light. Melatonin production peaks in early childhood and then sharply declines with age. Research shows melatonin levels average around 72 picograms per milliliter (pg/mL) in your mid-20s but can fall to about 25 pg/mL by age 80, often contributing to sleep difficulties experienced by older adults.

While melatonin supplements can assist with falling asleep or resetting disrupted sleep cycles (such as jet lag or shift work), they generally offer only modest improvements in overall sleep quality. Optimal supplementation involves low doses (0.5mg–2mg) taken 30–60 minutes before bedtime, with higher doses often leading to next-day grogginess.

For long-term sleep health, naturally enhancing melatonin production through good sleep hygiene is most effective:

- **Morning Sunlight Exposure:** Exposure to morning sunlight (blue light) resets your internal clock and boosts daytime alertness.

- **Evening Red Light Exposure:** In the evening, red or amber spectrum lighting promotes melatonin production and signals your body to wind down.

- **Screen Management:** Limit screen use 1–2 hours before bedtime or use blue-light-blocking glasses.

- **Consistency:** Maintain regular sleep-wake times each day, varying by no more than 30 minutes.

- **Bedroom Environment:** Keep your bedroom cool, dark, and quiet to support optimal sleep conditions.

- **Stress Reduction:** Engage in calming activities before bed to reduce stress, enhancing melatonin production and sleep quality.

Aligning your daily routine, exercise, meals, and cognitively demanding tasks, with these natural rhythms can significantly boost productivity, physical performance, and sleep quality, supporting your long-term health and longevity.

Sleep Mindset: Your Most Important Job

Think of sleep as your most important job. Just like showing up to work prepared and on time, your nightly rest demands a similar commitment. Establish clear routines that help you consistently "clock in" every night because your health and overall performance depend on it.

The quality of your sleep sets the tone for everything else in your life. You carefully design your workspace for productivity by removing distractions; similarly, your evening routine should be structured for maximum restfulness. Dim the lights, step away from screens, and take time to quiet your mind. Protect this time fiercely, because how you show up for sleep determines how effectively you'll show up everywhere else in life.

Mining Reward: Clock in for Sleep

Treat sleep like your most important job. Clock in on time, every night. No excuses. Quality sleep boosts your biological hashrate, optimizing your energy and productivity.

Sleep Apnea and Snoring:

Snoring and sleep apnea significantly disrupt restorative sleep, increase inflammation, and elevate the risk of serious conditions like cardiovascular disease and metabolic disorders. Untreated sleep apnea can even be life-threatening. If you or your partner regularly snores or experiences breathing interruptions at night, it's crucial to consult a healthcare provider for proper testing and diagnosis.

Newer wearables, like recent Apple Watch models, can help identify symptoms early, and advanced mattresses can detect snoring and automatically elevate your head to improve airflow and sleep quality. Today, these technologies serve as helpful indicators and supportive tools. Soon, with ongoing advancements, they might become accurate enough to diagnose sleep apnea as reliably as professional medical evaluations. Until then, always prioritize professional diagnosis and treatment if you suspect sleep apnea.

My Sleep Stack (Built Through Tracking and Experimentation)

So here's my real-life Layer 1, my foundation for consistently great sleep:

- **Morning Light Exposure:** Immediately upon waking, I expose my eyes to natural sunlight. If it's dark, I use a daylight or blue-light device. This sets my daily circadian rhythm and helps significantly improve mood and energy levels, particularly useful for combating Seasonal Affective Disorder (SAD).

- **Diet and Nutrition:** Eating nutrient-dense, anti-inflammatory foods throughout the day profoundly influences sleep quality. I avoid sugar, alcohol, and especially caffeine after 12 PM. Caffeine has a half-life of about 5–6 hours, so even afternoon coffee can linger in your system and disrupt sleep. I've noticed that gluten consumed after noon noticeably diminishes my sleep quality. Everyone's different, so it's critical to experiment and track your responses.

- **Exercise & Daily Movement:** Exercise has a clear impact on sleep quality. If I skip my daily 10,000 steps or miss a workout, it's harder to fall asleep and stay asleep. Consistent daily activity is crucial for achieving deep, restorative sleep.

Closer to bedtime, my routine involves:

- **Early Dinner:** I stop eating by 4 PM, adhering to a 16:8 fasting schedule. If I eat anything after 4 PM, I notice a meaningful reduction in sleep quality. Eating early improves my deep sleep and lowers my resting heart rate at bedtime, helping me fall asleep faster.

- **Blue Light Blocking Glasses:** From 6:30 PM onwards, I wear blue light blocking glasses to protect my circadian rhythm.

- **Hot Shower:** Around 1–2 hours before bedtime, I take a hot shower to help lower my core body temperature, signaling my body it's time for sleep.

- **Screens Off by 7:30 PM:** I turn off all screens by 7:30 PM to ensure my mind can fully calm down before sleep.

- **Supplements (30–60 minutes before bed):**
  - Magnesium Glycinate: 100–300 mg
  - Glycine Powder: 1.5–3 grams

- **Wind-down Routine:** My routine includes reading, breathwork, meditation, or a gentle walk. No stress allowed. Anything on my mind is noted for "morning me" to handle.

- **Red Light Bulb:** Using red or amber lighting in the evening helps maintain melatonin levels and signals my body it's time for sleep.

- **Cool Bedroom Environment:** I sleep on a temperature-controlled mattress with automated cooling (60–68°F) to promote deeper, uninterrupted sleep, along with a grounding sheet. My data tracking confirms that grounding boosts nighttime heart rate variability (HRV) and next-day recovery. My bed also detects snoring and gently elevates the head to improve airflow and minimize disturbances, especially helpful if your partner tends to snore.

- **Dark Room:** Ensuring complete darkness optimizes melatonin production and deep sleep. I use blackout curtains and minimize all artificial light sources.

- **Consistent Bedtime:** In bed by 8:30 PM, asleep by 9 PM to maximize deep sleep before 2 AM (when it's physiologically hardest to achieve). While some deep sleep can occur after 2 a.m., your biological clock strongly favors earlier bedtimes for optimal deep sleep and recovery.

Power Naps

If you didn't get enough sleep, a short daytime nap can be incredibly helpful for restoring energy and cognitive performance. Research shows that power naps can reduce fatigue, improve memory, sharpen focus, and even partially compensate for lost sleep at night.

Life often gets in the way of a perfect night's sleep. Traveling across time zones, caring for babies or small children, or working late can disrupt your sleep patterns. Personally, I frequently travel for night photography and sunrise shoots, requiring me to stay up late or wake at odd hours. I've found that taking short naps helps significantly to offset these disruptions and maintain my energy and mental clarity. During college, 20-minute power naps became my survival strategy between classes and work shifts.

When taking a power nap during the day, listening to theta waves helps me fall asleep quickly. Theta waves are a type of brainwave associated with relaxation, deep meditation, and the transition between wakefulness and sleep. They generally range between 4 and 8 Hz and are closely linked to learning and memory formation. You can easily find theta wave tracks on YouTube or streaming platforms.

For a quick energy boost, I aim for about 20–30 minutes. Any longer than that risks waking up groggy, as you might interrupt a deeper sleep cycle. If you have the time, a full 90-minute nap can allow you to complete an entire sleep cycle, leaving you refreshed and avoiding drowsiness.

Some of my best ideas come right before I fall asleep. Always write these down immediately; never let them slip away. Many insights for this book emerged between 2 AM and 4 AM, when I'm half-awake between sleep cycles. While noting these down might temporarily disrupt sleep, sometimes... it's worth it.

My Deep Sleep Elixir Recipe

Ingredients:

- 100–300 mg Magnesium Glycinate

- 1.5–3 grams (g) Glycine Powder

- Optional: Lemon balm or chamomile tea

Instructions:

1. Take Magnesium Glycinate in pill form as directed.

2. Dissolve Glycine Powder into a small amount of water or your preferred beverage, using just enough liquid to fully dissolve the powder. *(Optional: If desired, steep lemon balm or chamomile tea and use this as your liquid base.)*

3. Drink the elixir 30–60 minutes before bedtime to calm your nervous system, boost GABA (your brain's calming neurotransmitter), and promote muscle relaxation.

4. Keep the liquid volume minimal to avoid nighttime awakenings and support uninterrupted sleep.

Tofu Scramble Recipe

Serves: 2

Start your morning off right. This tofu scramble is my favorite breakfast. I probably eat it four days a week. Packed with anti-inflammatory nutrients and healthy fats, it stabilizes blood sugar, provides sustained energy, and helps regulate your circadian rhythm. Eating nutrient-dense, anti-inflammatory meals early in the day primes your body for better sleep at night.

Ingredients:

- ½ medium onion, diced

- 1 medium sweet potato, cubed small

- 2–3 cups seasonal organic veggies, chopped *(zucchini, kale, broccoli, cauliflower, peppers, whatever's fresh)*

- 8 oz firm tofu *(about half a standard 16 oz. package)*, drained and crumbled

- ½ teaspoon turmeric *(helps reduce inflammation, promoting better sleep quality)*

- Pinch of black pepper *(enhances turmeric absorption)*

- 1 tablespoon nutritional yeast *(rich in B vitamins to support stress reduction and restful sleep)*

- Coconut oil

- Extra virgin olive oil

- ½ avocado, sliced

- Spicy sriracha sauce *(optional, but highly recommended)*

Instructions:

1. Heat about 1 tablespoon of coconut oil in a skillet over medium heat.

2. Cook sweet potatoes until golden and tender (about 8–10 minutes).

3. Add diced onions and sauté until translucent, about 2–3 minutes.

4. Add seasonal vegetables and cook for an additional 5 minutes, until crisp-tender.

5. Crumble tofu into the pan, turn off the heat, and gently stir to combine.

6. Sprinkle with turmeric, black pepper, and nutritional yeast. Drizzle lightly with extra virgin olive oil and gently stir again.

7. Divide into two portions, top each with avocado slices, and finish with a generous drizzle of spicy sriracha sauce.

Bitcoin Recipe: Lightning Wallet Setup

Let's layer up. As you optimize your biological base layer of sleep and build upper layers, such as specialized dietary strategies, targeted exercise, and advanced lifestyle habits, ensure you're also strengthening your financial layers. Bitcoin forms your foundational financial layer, providing security, decentralization, and immutability. Now let's move up to financial Layer 2 with the Lightning Network, enabling instant, low-cost transactions. I'll show you how to set up a Lightning wallet and send sats instantly.

Ingredients:

- Smartphone

Instructions:

1. Outside the U.S.:

   - Download Wallet of Satoshi for instant Lightning payments. (At the time of writing, Wallet of Satoshi anticipates being available in the U.S. again in 2025.)

2. Inside the U.S.:

   - Download Aqua Wallet, which supports Lightning (Layer 2) and Liquid (Layer 3) for privacy, speed, and flexibility.

3. Fund your wallet, then send a few sats to a friend or tip your favorite content creator and experience firsthand the speed and convenience of Bitcoin's Layer 2.

Feeling adventurous? Run a Lightning node. To fully harness Lightning's capabilities, you'll need to run your own Bitcoin node before setting up a Lightning node. Plug-and-play solutions like *Umbrel, Start9,* and *MyNode* simplify this process. Once you're set up, connect your node to *Zeus* (zeusln. com), a user-friendly app that lets you send and receive Bitcoin directly from your own node using your phone. Plebnet (plebnetwiki.com) has great resources for getting started.

Bonus Recipe: Set Up a Nostr Account

Ready for a decentralized, open-source social media protocol that integrates seamlessly with Lightning for instant value transactions?

Ingredients:

- Smartphone or computer

- Secure storage for keys (password manager, encrypted drive, or hardware device)

Instructions:

1. Create your Nostr keys:

   - Download a Nostr client such as Primal, Damus, or Amethyst, then securely generate your public/private key pair.

   - SECURELY back up your private/public key. If you lose this, you lose access to your account.

2. Fund your wallet:

   - Link your Lightning wallet to instantly zap sats to posts you appreciate. You can also directly send sats to any user on Nostr, enabling seamless peer-to-peer value transfer.

3. Start posting and zapping:

   - Experience a censorship-resistant social network with instant, frictionless value exchange

Chapter 7

Resilience & Antifragility: How to Build an Unbreakable Life

I sold my first iPhone for $200, just enough to fill my car with diesel and stay in a few questionable motel rooms. It was a tough goodbye; that phone had been a generous gift from an incredible boss at Miss Universe, and my first smartphone ever. But practicality outweighed sentimentality. $200 would stretch me from Ohio to California in my beat-up VW Bug, affectionately named Ringo (you know, because it was a Beatle). Ringo wasn't much to look at, a patchwork of mismatched panels and salvaged parts, but he was my lifeline. I loved that car.

On a muggy May morning in 2012, I shoved my belongings into Ringo, along with peanut butter and jelly sandwiches, juice boxes, and a precious stack of vintage Bon Jovi cassettes snagged from eBay for a few dollars (Figure 13). It felt like the most important game of Tetris I'd ever played: anything that didn't fit had to stay behind. Sitting in the driver's seat, hot leather searing my thighs every time I shifted positions, I shuffled the printed MapQuest directions, their edges already curling from the heat. Ringo had no air conditioning, no working windows, and no power steering. Just shifting gears required muscling the clutch with a cramped leg, one hand jerking the gear shift while cranking the heavy wheel with the other. Sweat soaked through my tank top before I even pulled away from the curb. But there was no turning back.

The road west stretched endlessly, shimmering under relentless heat. My black Bug quickly turned into a personal sauna, trapping every ounce of humidity. I learned to touch the metal shifter and e-brake in quick taps, like testing a hot pan. Every toll booth brought a small humiliation. Since my

windows didn't open, I had to stop, kick open the creaky door, climb out
to pay, endure puzzled stares from attendants, then scramble back into the
scorching interior and keep moving.

It's profound how clearly you think when there's no safety net beneath you.
With everything riding on my success, my survival instinct sharpened into
breathtaking intensity. My mind was singularly focused: You're making it.
Each moment stretched vividly, every tiny detail hyper-real, the hum of tires
on blistering asphalt, the crackling of the cassette player barely masking the
persistent road noise, white-knuckling the wheel as Ringo got blown around
on the freeway, jolted by passing semi-trucks and gusts of wind.

Kansas was brutal: a flat, desolate landscape of emptiness that seemed to
mock my progress. It was during this relentless stretch of highway that I first
heard Bon Jovi's "Dry County."

The opening lines felt hauntingly fitting:

> "Across the border, they turn water into wine
> Some say it's the devil's blood they're squeezing from the vine
> Some say it's a saviour in these hard and desperate times
> You see, it helps me to forget that we're just born to die
> I came here like so many did, to find the better life
> To find my piece of easy street, to finally be alive
> And I knew nothing good comes easy
> All good things take some time."

I must have replayed the song forty times, each repetition underscoring how
painfully slow I was traveling. Time stood still. I genuinely began wonder-
ing if Kansas had some supernatural power to trap travelers in an eternal
loop. Every creak from Ringo made my heart skip, each sputter a terrifying
reminder of how alone I truly was. The reality was stark: if Ringo died, I
had nowhere to turn.

But then I reminded myself: at least I wasn't stranded in the Amazon or lost
in the chaos of India. If I broke down, eventually, someone would pass by.
There would always be a way forward. Compared to those previous struggles, this felt manageable, almost easy. That quick shift in perspective helped
steady my nerves and kept me driving forward, reinforcing my determination with every mile. My mental game had never been sharper. Every time
exhaustion or doubt crept in, I vividly imagined the cool relief of California's ocean air, my hands releasing their grip on the hot wheel, and my tired
body finally relaxing as I reached my destination. Each time this vision

faded, I channeled every ounce of negativity and doubt I'd absorbed from my family. Their disbelief became my determination. Every mile became a small victory, a tangible rejection of the place that had tried to dictate who I was allowed to become. My anger toward Ohio became the fuel propelling Ringo steadily, stubbornly westward. It might not have been healthy, but it worked.

Relief came in brief, bright bursts. Friends in Illinois and Colorado welcomed me warmly, offering hot showers, good meals, laughter, and competitive rounds of Just Dance. After days sealed inside Ringo's suffocating heat, stepping into their air-conditioned homes felt almost magical. Every encouraging word briefly lifted the weight of isolation, making the long hours on empty highways just a bit easier.

During the long stretches between these visits, reality hit hardest. This journey represented more than miles traveled; it symbolized breaking free from a comfort trap I'd lived in for far too long. I was deliberately stepping into uncertainty, discomfort, and risk because instinctively I knew that's where personal growth occurs. Years later, when I left the winery job waiting for me in California, I'd explicitly tell myself, "Don't give yourself the option to fail." But it was on this blistering road beneath a relentless summer sun that I first truly understood what those words meant.

When everything rides on your success, when your only choices are to succeed or face homelessness, you discover resilience you never knew existed. You become unstoppable, resourceful, and determined in ways that surprise even you. Your mindset sharpens: waste no opportunities. When your moment appears, you ride.

Figure 13. Images of cross-country road trip taken May 2012 by Erin E. Malone.

Stuck in the Comfort Trap

We are creatures of habit. From the moment we wake up, our days often unfold predictably. We have identical morning routines, the same commutes, repetitive tasks at work, recurring casual conversations, and mind-numbing TV shows in the evening. This predictability provides a sense of comfort and security, but quietly numbs our minds and shrinks our perception of time without us even realizing it.

Over a century ago, psychologist William James captured this phenomenon vividly in *The Principles of Psychology*. James noted that new experiences embed themselves deeply into our memories, slowing our perception of time and enriching our sense of life. In contrast, habitual routines pass unnoticed, blending seamlessly into one another, making days, weeks, and even years feel indistinct, what he described as "hollowed-out."

Modern research continues to confirm James's insights. A team of Israeli scientists studying time perception found that people consistently underestimate the duration of routine tasks compared to new experiences. Simply put, our brains are built to prioritize novelty. When we're engaged in something new or unpredictable, we snap out of autopilot mode. We become present, alert, and vividly aware. Time slows down again, and our days and years become richer, fuller, and more memorable. This is exactly why time seemed to pass slowly during childhood, when every experience was fresh, new, and full of wonder.

Yet contemporary life has largely erased this newness. Convenience culture, technological comforts, and predictable routines keep us sheltered in comfort. In 2024, nearly 61 percent of American TV consumers spent three or more hours per day watching TV. The average American watched approximately two and a half hours of television daily, with older adults averaging even higher numbers. When asked why they don't pursue healthier or more meaningful activities, many say they're simply too tired or overwhelmed from work.

The average U.S. adult now spends over seven hours per day on screens. This total screen time surpasses the global average, positioning the U.S. among the top countries for digital consumption. Ironically, the comfortable routine of mindless screen time each day, intended as downtime, often turns into hours spent doom-scrolling, spiraling in chaos, and hooked on addictive algorithms. This further drains energy and motivation, creating a cycle of comfort that traps people deeper in fatigue, complacency, and perceived busyness.

Beyond individual harm, this comfort trap quietly erodes our connections to one another. Hours lost to passive entertainment replace opportunities for meaningful interactions with friends, family, and community, connections proven to enhance our longevity. Later, we'll expand on how strong communities in Blue Zones profoundly improve their residents' longevity and overall well-being.

If we genuinely want to live longer, not just in years, but in richer, more fulfilling experiences, we must break out of our comfort traps. We must deliberately seek discomfort. Discomfort forces growth. Growth fuels resilience. And resilience is the foundation upon which our future selves depend.

Breaking the Trance: Why New Experiences Matter

Seeking new experiences is essential fuel for our cognitive and emotional health. Embracing new experiences creates lasting memories and actively stimulates our brain's capacity for adaptation, growth, and resilience.

Think back to childhood. The days felt long. The summers were endless. Each year brought significant milestones and distinct memories because so much of our world was unexplored. Our brains thrived on this constant stream of new experiences. Each of these vivid moments was deeply etched into our memories. But as adults, repetition and predictability begin to dull that sharp perception. Routine doesn't just blur our days; it quiets our minds, reduces emotional vibrancy, and dampens our ability to adapt to stress and change.

Recent neuroscience research shows exactly why seeking new experiences is so important. Encountering something new triggers the release of dopamine, a neurotransmitter linked not only to pleasure but also motivation, learning, and memory formation. Frequent exposure to new experiences strengthens neural pathways, builds cognitive reserve, and enhances neuroplasticity, the brain's ability to reorganize itself by forming new connections. Consistently seeking new experiences literally builds new pathways in your brain, strengthening it and helping you remain sharp, resilient, and adaptable as you age. Research consistently shows that lifelong learners experience significantly lower rates of dementia.

Beyond brain chemistry, new experiences involve perception and engagement. When every day looks and feels the same, our minds drift into autopilot. New experiences disrupt this trance, pulling us sharply into the present moment. Colors seem brighter, scents become memorable, and sounds resonate more clearly. They force us into active engagement with our environment, igniting curiosity and sharpening our focus.

This is precisely why incorporating new experiences into our daily lives is so powerful. Whether it's as significant as climbing a mountain, entering your first race, traveling to a new city, or simply joining a new social group, seeking something new reconnects us with the experience of living vividly and deeply. It reawakens the clarity, curiosity, and wonder we knew as children, making life feel exciting again and sharpening our minds for improved cognitive health, emotional resilience, and overall longevity.

If you really want to future-proof your life, new experiences need to be actively sought out and intentionally woven into your daily routine. As we'll explore in upcoming sections, breaking free from the comfort trap doesn't require drastic change overnight. It's about consistently choosing small, meaningful shifts toward adventure, exploration, and growth. Sometimes it's simply about saying yes.

Cognitive Fitness: Building Your Mind Through Experience

Today, we often shy away from difficult or uncomfortable tasks. We skip workouts, avoid tough conversations, or put off learning new skills. Each time we take the easy route, we weaken our ability to handle life's inevitable challenges and usually end up making things harder for ourselves in the long run.

I learned early to lean directly into discomfort. During my Miss Universe internship, every setback or stressful moment became a lesson. Challenges taught me clarity, like realizing a corporate office job wasn't the path for me. Sometimes learning what you don't want is just as important as knowing what you do. Every difficult moment taught me empathy, resilience, and the value of treating each experience as an opportunity to grow. Between 2016 and 2022, some of my greatest lessons came from adventures near or above the Arctic Circle, chasing northern lights, sailing beneath Greenland's midnight sun, photographing wolverines in Finland, exploring northern Norway, and enduring Icelandic hurricanes and Faroese hailstorms. These trips were brutally cold, sleep-deprived, and physically exhausting...and they were also some of the absolute best times of my life (Figure 14).

I typically traveled with a few photographers from around the world, and every frozen night, every grueling climb, every storm we weathered strengthened our resilience. It was brutal, but each moment reinforced one idea: the most rewarding experiences come from embracing challenges head-on. Every time, we'd look at each other and say, "Worth it!"

Rich Experiences Create Richer Minds

Real-world adventures shape your mind in ways that just can't be replicated by theoretical knowledge alone. Like landing drones on moving ships in Greenland, troubleshooting unexpected problems and equipment failures in remote locations (ever dodge a frozen drone falling out of the sky?), and pushing through physical exhaustion taught me adaptability, creativity, and patience under pressure. Even on my journey to California, the drive from Colorado onward felt like stepping into a painting, each mile revealing snow-capped peaks and the stunning, surreal beauty of Utah's salt flats stretching endlessly toward the horizon. The landscape seemed impossibly vast and bright, a dazzling expanse that felt like a visual reward after enduring Kansas. These vivid scenes etched themselves into my memory, marking how dramatically my surroundings had changed since leaving Ohio.

The real payoff of these experiences is that they make you a more interesting person. They expand your perspective and connect you deeply with others. Some of the strongest friendships of my life formed in these challenging conditions. The bonds formed beneath the northern lights after days spent hunting them (yes, it's called hunting), listening to whales singing beside your boat at 3 am in Greenland, or waiting out a snowstorm around a fire, sharing warm drinks and stories, or sometimes even a late-night Just Dance battle after driving for twelve straight hours to Illinois, those moments stick with you forever.

 Mining Reward: Difficulty Builds Strength

Bitcoin adjusts its difficulty based on network strength. Life works the same: embrace tough challenges as difficulty adjustments. Each challenge you overcome makes your personal network stronger.

Figure 14: Images from Norway, Iceland, Finland, Faroe Islands, and Greenland, taken from 2016-2022 by Erin E. Malone.

The People Who Shape You

Travel is as much about the people you meet as the places you go. During my last trip to Finland, we arrived in a tiny northern town near the Finnish-Russian border just as Russia began mobilizing troops for its invasion of Ukraine. The Russian-operated car rental company we booked with abruptly shut down, leaving us stranded without refunds or transportation. Through friends of friends, a local we'd never met immediately offered us his family car for the week, no questions asked. He simply handed us the keys. We dropped him off at his house, planned a time and place to return the car, and continued our journey. The trust and generosity of the Finns created a ripple effect of kindness that lasted throughout our journey and stayed with me long after the trip ended.

In Lofoten, Norway, I traveled with five photographers I'd connected with through Instagram. This was 2016, and none of us had ever met in person before. Two people came from France, two from Sweden, one from Finland, and then me. Was it safe or smart to travel to the top of the world with strangers from the internet? Who knew? But at the time, Instagram felt like an exciting new way to connect internationally with others who shared your passion. We spent our days traveling between islands, hiking, photographing stunning landscapes, and hunting for the Northern Lights. After four days together, a sudden snowstorm confined us to our cabin. It happened to be Bree's birthday, one of the Swedes. We had carried only our small camera backpacks, so we were astonished when Réza, our exuberant French leader, suddenly pulled out two bottles of champagne from his bag. How long had he hidden them there? There hadn't exactly been convenient champagne stops along the way. As we laughed and toasted, Réza also produced a tiny disco ball that synced to music, along with a portable speaker. Our cozy cabin quickly transformed into a spontaneous party, a French rave in the middle of nowhere. Alex, the other Frenchman, didn't speak any English; we had been translating for each other the entire trip. Yet that night, Alex revealed he had memorized a series of incredibly dirty jokes in perfect English. His flawless, hilarious delivery had us all laughing until we cried. Moments like these forge lasting friendships and create memories that never fade. Since then, I never travel without a disco ball.

Later that same year, I traveled to Iceland with two friends from the Lofoten trip. We spent several exhausting days traversing rugged terrain in a Defender, one of the coolest yet toughest vehicles, reaching some of the most remote regions at the very top of the country, at 66 degrees north near the Arctic Circle. After five days of intense travel, battling hurricane-force winds and unpredictable weather, we were thoroughly worn down. Eventually, a magical hot spring appeared in the middle of nowhere. Slipping into the warm water, we finally relaxed and looked up to see the northern lights dancing brilliantly above us. Exchanging silent glances, each of us debated whether to grab a camera. Without speaking, we unanimously decided the moment was too magical to disrupt. It remains the best display of Northern Lights I've ever experienced, made unforgettable by sharing it with friends who soon became longtime travel companions.

Small gestures often have the greatest impact: the truck driver in Utah offering me a can of nuts to feed wild prairie dogs, friends opening their homes along my drive, or the coworker who let me stay with her my first week in California until I found my own place. When I graduated from high school, a coworker at the same grocery store I worked at gave me $50 as a graduation gift. At that time, money was so tight that this small gesture allowed me to eat for several weeks. Nearly twenty years later, I still think about how much that thoughtful gesture meant to me. Each of these moments reinforced how powerful and uplifting genuine kindness can be, especially during challenging times Inspired by these experiences, I always strive to pay it forward whenever possible. You never know when one small act might profoundly change someone's life.

Embrace Discomfort, Grow Intentionally

Ultimately, cognitive fitness requires intentionally seeking out situations that challenge your mind and push your comfort level. Facing the extremes in the Arctic and being stranded for days in the Amazon rainforest taught me firsthand that true growth happens when you're pushed to your limits in some of the most unforgiving environments. These moments also make life feel a little more vivid, sharpening your senses and deepening your appreciation for the world around you.

Choosing intentional discomfort regularly prepares you for future challenges, enriching your life in ways comfort simply can't. The more you embrace these experiences, the stronger, more adaptable, and more capable you become.

Antifragility: The Longevity Advantage of Discomfort

Comfort is warm, safe, reassuring, and...temporary. If our aim is true longevity and vitality, comfort alone won't get us there. This is where Nassim Taleb's book, *Antifragile*, offers a powerful framework for rethinking stress and discomfort.

Taleb describes antifragility as the opposite of fragility. Fragile things break under stress, robust things merely endure it, but antifragile things actually grow stronger. Consider your muscles: lifting weights initially stresses and slightly damages muscle fibers, but your body responds by repairing and rebuilding them even stronger.

Your bones adapt similarly. The impact from weight-bearing activities like walking, running, and resistance training directly stimulates bones, prompting them to become denser and more resilient. Many older adults choose lower-impact exercises such as swimming or cycling, which are excellent for cardiovascular health. However, because these activities lack the beneficial impact of weight-bearing exercises, they don't effectively trigger the bone-strengthening process. Regular, controlled physical stress is essential, especially as we age. Osteoporosis has multiple factors, but insufficient weight-bearing activity can significantly accelerate bone-density loss, which can increase vulnerability to fractures.

Biologically, this adaptive response to beneficial stress is known as **hormesis**, a phenomenon where moderate exposure to stress triggers the body to grow stronger. Small, controlled doses of stress activate specific cellular and metabolic processes, such as reducing inflammation, boosting antioxidant defenses, repairing damaged proteins, and enhancing immune function. Practices like intermittent fasting, cold exposure, sauna sessions, and high-intensity exercise all rely on hormesis. They might feel uncomfortable in the moment, but over time, they profoundly improve your body's ability to handle stress by literally making your cells healthier, tougher, and more resilient. However, these practices aren't suitable for everyone. If you have underlying health conditions or specific medical concerns, always consult a healthcare professional before experimenting with hormetic stressors.

Antifragility extends into our mental, emotional, and even financial lives. Regularly confronting manageable stressors, such as learning new skills, pushing beyond comfort zones, and navigating uncertainty, builds profound internal resilience. Over time, we not only cope better with life's inevitable setbacks but also actively benefit from them. For instance, a job loss, while initially stressful, pushes you out of your comfort zone. It might inspire you to launch a new business, eventually leading to greater fulfillment, financial independence, and personal growth.

In other words, the path to longevity is paved with deliberate discomfort, intentional stress, and mindful challenge. Embracing antifragility means consciously choosing physical, mental, and financial challenges as essential investments, knowing that today's discomfort directly translates into tomorrow's strength, resilience, and lasting health.

Mindset as Longevity Medicine

Your mindset shapes more than your outlook on life. It directly impacts your biology, influencing everything from stress hormones to inflammation and cardiovascular health, ultimately determining how long and how well you live.

Dr. Carol Dweck, a renowned psychologist and researcher at Stanford University, introduced the world to two powerful ways of viewing challenges and potential: a **fixed mindset** and a **growth mindset**. A fixed mindset views abilities and intelligence as largely predetermined; you're either good at something or you're not. Challenges become threats because they risk revealing your limitations. In contrast, a growth mindset sees abilities as flexible and improvable. Challenges become opportunities to learn, grow, and adapt.

This mindset difference deeply impacts your biology. Research consistently shows that people who embrace challenges and view stress positively have lower cortisol levels, reduced inflammation, better cardiovascular health, and stronger immune responses. Optimism and a growth-oriented mindset actively program our biology for longevity by influencing daily behaviors like nutrition, exercise, and stress management.

Cultivating a growth mindset involves reframing your internal dialogue. Replace thoughts of *"I can't"* or *"I'm not good at this"* with phrases like *"I'm still learning," "This is challenging, but I'm improving,"* or, as I often say, *"I'll figure this out."* This simple reframing powerfully reshapes how your brain responds to stress, fostering a biological environment conducive to longevity.

Regularly choosing challenges that push you just beyond your comfort zone can reinforce your internal narrative of growth and capability. Personally, I've found that successfully completing a difficult task provides an immediate rush of satisfaction and momentum, motivating me to seek out even more challenges. Traveling and experiencing new things fuels my desire to explore further. Reading something interesting inspires me to dive deeper into learning. This positive feedback loop continually strengthens your growth mindset and deepens your engagement with life.

Yet today, many of us habitually avoid tasks we perceive as difficult or uncomfortable. We seek comfort and predictability instead of building our problem-solving muscles. Unfortunately, avoiding challenging situations doesn't just weaken our minds; it weakens our biology. Each avoided challenge is a missed opportunity for growth, resilience, and improved longevity. Sometimes growth means simply saying yes. Other times, it means intentionally saying no to the easier path and choosing the more challenging one, not because it's harder, but because it will help you improve and grow. Even on this path, remember you can still work smarter, not harder, by creating efficient systems, developing new skills, or strategically approaching your goals.

Despite having limitless information at our fingertips, we often struggle to engage deeply or solve problems from first principles, breaking down issues into fundamental truths to build understanding from the ground up. Instead of slowing down and using deeper analytical thinking, we frequently default to shortcuts and quick fixes driven by a high time preference. For example, we might just skim a headline or quickly scan a social media blurb instead of reading the full article or seeking additional context. Or instead of researching how to fix something by watching a quick YouTube tutorial, we immediately buy a replacement (Right to Repair is a growing movement that is challenging this trend). We choose immediate, surface-level comfort over long-term understanding and growth. But constantly avoiding deeper thinking limits our adaptability, weakens our problem-solving, and keeps us from meaningful learning.

This might actually reflect a broader cultural issue. Alarmingly, recent studies show that approximately 54% of American adults aged 16–74 have literacy skills below a sixth-grade level. This suggests widespread difficulty in engaging with complex, nuanced information, skills that are critical for effective decision-making, problem-solving, and personal growth. Perhaps we've reached a critical reflection point, offering us the opportunity to reconsider our approach as a species and actively seek deeper understanding and improvement.

Ultimately, your mindset acts as your body's biological instruction manual. A growth mindset programs resilience, adaptability, and longevity. Your beliefs and attitudes literally shape your physical future. By intentionally cultivating a growth-oriented mindset, you're actively shaping your perspective of the world and directly influencing how your body responds to it.

Just as your mindset shapes your health and longevity, it significantly impacts your approach to money. Adopting a growth-oriented perspective leads you naturally toward financial strategies that strengthen resilience and adaptability.

Your mindset is your greatest tool for longevity, wellness, and financial freedom.

Mining Reward: Right to Repair Your Mindset

The Right to Repair movement encourages reclaiming skills to fix and maintain devices instead of immediately buying replacements. Choosing repair fosters lifelong learning, adaptability, and resilience, equipping you to solve problems and remain financially and personally self-reliant.

Bitcoin and Financial Antifragility

To build wealth that withstands economic shocks, and even thrives during uncertainty, you need financial antifragility. Bitcoin uniquely embodies this principle, offering a powerful way to create financial resilience and adaptability.

Bitcoin's design embodies Nassim Taleb's concept of antifragility. Traditional financial systems are fragile antiques: centralized, overly complex, and prone to catastrophic failures under stress. We've repeatedly seen financial institutions crumble, leaving billions economically stranded. Bitcoin, however, thrives during uncertainty. Its decentralized structure, censorship resistance, and transparent, fixed monetary rules (capped forever at just 21 million coins) allow it to grow stronger as trust in traditional finance weakens.

Every day, Bitcoin's global adoption grows, reinforcing its antifragile properties. Distributed miners secure the network worldwide, ensuring no single entity can dominate its operation. Individuals running nodes, businesses innovating with Bitcoin-based products, and developers actively reviewing its code all contribute to its ongoing resilience. Over time, despite volatility, crashes, and regulatory challenges, Bitcoin has consistently emerged stronger, increasing in value and global significance.

A striking example of Bitcoin's antifragility was the Chinese mining ban in May 2021. China had previously hosted over half of the global Bitcoin mining power. When the ban was enacted, Bitcoin's hashrate dropped sharply as miners quickly shut down or relocated operations to friendlier jurisdictions such as the U.S., Kazakhstan, and Canada. However, reports emerged soon after the ban that several underground mining operations remained active within China. Remarkably, within six months, Bitcoin's hashrate made a full, V-shaped recovery, returning stronger and more geographically dispersed than before. Despite China's attempt to ban mining, within six months, the country had regained around 22% of global mining power. Such attempts at suppression highlight Bitcoin's incredible resilience. Banning Bitcoin causes jurisdictions to sacrifice direct financial benefits as well as crucial second-order advantages, including improved energy production, infrastructure investment, and grid stabilization, ultimately driving away economic and intellectual capital.

Another pivotal event showcasing Bitcoin's antifragility was the Block Size Wars between 2015 and 2017. During this period, the community faced intense debate over the best way to scale Bitcoin. "Large blockers" pushed for bigger blocks that could handle more transactions per block, but this approach would make running a node more expensive, limiting participation to those who could afford powerful hardware. "Small blockers," in contrast, preferred solutions like Segregated Witness (SegWit) and the Lightning Network, which allowed scaling through second-layer technologies without sacrificing decentralization. In the end, decentralized consensus prevailed. Bitcoin kept smaller blocks, ensuring anyone could run a node, which preserved the network's decentralization and accessibility. This outcome strengthened Bitcoin's long-term resilience and adaptability without compromising its core principles.

Holding Bitcoin protects your wealth while fundamentally reshaping your relationship with money. It shifts your financial perspective away from short-term gains and high time preference toward a deliberate focus on long-term growth, discipline, and self-sovereignty. Like muscles or bones strengthened by beneficial stress, financial discipline gained from experiencing Bitcoin's ups and downs strengthens your economic resilience, teaching patience and strategic thinking.

Adopting Bitcoin encourages financial literacy and critical thinking. Bitcoin holders must actively engage, learn how the ecosystem works, understand economic principles, and manage self-custody responsibly. Each of these experiences reinforces deeper understanding, accountability, and intentionality, directly fostering an antifragile financial mindset.

You don't have to go all-in overnight. Instead, you can accumulate Bitcoin steadily over time through **dollar-cost averaging** (consistently buying small amounts regularly). This approach helps mitigate volatility and steadily builds resilience. As you learn more and experience how disciplined financial actions directly lead to long-term savings and stability, your confidence and competence naturally grow.

Bitcoin is a proven pathway to economic antifragility and financial resilience. Just as you proactively seek physical stressors to future-proof your health, proactively embracing Bitcoin is an effective way to future-proof your financial health, giving you control, strength, and stability, even in uncertain economic conditions.

Experimentation as a Lifestyle

One night in the middle of the pandemic, a handful of passionate Bitcoiners gathered online. The Lightning Network was still new, and none of us really knew how to run a node, let alone make a routing node profitable. There were no guides, no tutorials, and no easy resources to follow. We stayed up late that first night on Clubhouse and Telegram, shared the little knowledge we had, and experimented through trial and error. We opened channels together, invented our own lingo, shared memes, and built friendships around a shared mission. What began as a tiny group of about fifteen quickly exploded into over 6,000 people within six months, becoming Plebnet, a thriving global network of Lightning node runners (Figure 15).

In the months and years that followed, we taught thousands how to run their own nodes, become their own banks, and route not just their own payments but the world's payments. By carefully managing channels and providing liquidity, we directly strengthened the Lightning Network itself. We documented our collective findings and made them freely accessible at *plebnetwiki.com* and through our Telegram group, which eventually gave rise to numerous specialized communities. When El Salvador adopted Bitcoin several months later, our community was ready. Our nodes routed payments, supported transactions, and demonstrated the real-world power of decentralized collaboration. (Also, I'm pretty sure Plebnet was responsible for a temporary global shortage of Raspberry Pis, the small computers many of us used to run our nodes.)

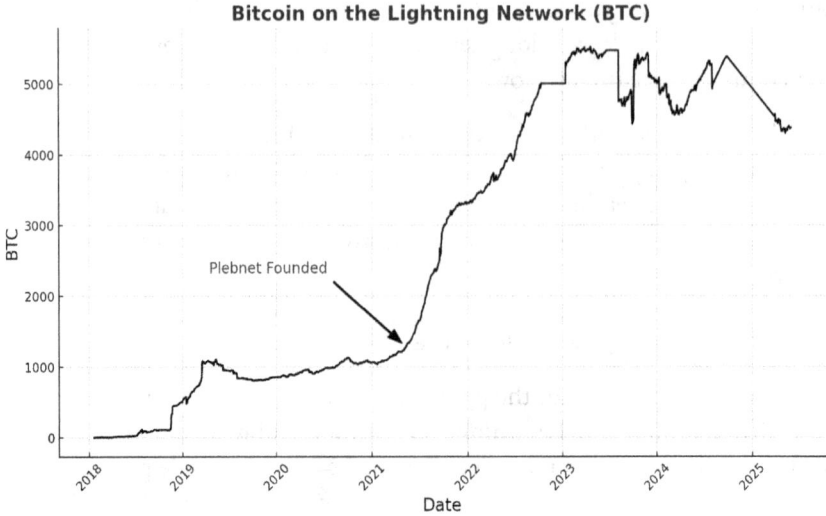

Figure 15: Lightning Network Capacity. (Bitcoin Visuals, https://bitcoinvisuals.com/ln-capacity). Chart created by Erin E. Malone.

This community-driven approach mirrors exactly how I tackle personal health optimization. Recently, I joined the longevity-focused community app "Don't Die," connecting with health-conscious people who ask thoughtful questions, share practical insights, and discuss results from their own experiments. Whether it's optimizing sleep, testing nutrition timing, or tracking biometrics, my approach stays consistent: start small, measure obsessively, adjust regularly, and leverage the collective intelligence of the community. Just as running a Lightning node requires precise channel management and regular fine-tuning, optimizing your health demands continuous experimentation, adaptation, and input from others who share your goals.

The same mindset fuels my curiosity about every aspect of Bitcoin. For example, I bought an ASIC miner just to deeply understand mining. I took it apart, put it back together, experimented with hash rates and efficiencies, and studied setups and results shared by other home miners. I also openly shared my own findings and experiences. Eventually, I even repurposed the miner's excess heat to warm my home and hot tub. I view tinkering as a mindset. It's how I engage with the world, how I explore possibilities, and ultimately, how I figure things out. When you combine ongoing experimentation with the collective intelligence of a committed community, your impact multiplies. You're not just gaining knowledge; you're actively solving problems, discovering what's possible, and maybe even changing the world.

Owning Your Struggle

The drive to experiment, adapt, and build resilience often emerges directly from your toughest experiences. Looking back, I realize something profound: had I grown up in a safe, nurturing, comfortable environment, I might never have found myself on that road to California. I might never have built the strength or resilience necessary to thrive in challenging conditions. I might never have needed Bitcoin, or felt the urgency to truly understand it. While I wouldn't wish hardship on anyone, there's transformative power in struggle. It's all about perspective.

Sometimes you need to make peace with past traumas, even let them fuel you. Negative experiences provide clarity about what's truly important and what's merely inconvenient. When you know what real hardship looks like, everyday setbacks become minor obstacles rather than existential crises. Embrace your struggles, use them. Let them shape you into someone stronger, wiser, and kinder. Or better yet, channel those experiences into making the world a more compassionate place, ensuring others have better opportunities than you did.

Resilience isn't just surviving tough situations. It's actively choosing to thrive because of them.

Practical Strategies: Seeking Daily Discomfort

You can gradually build resilience and antifragility without completely uprooting your life overnight. It's more about regularly introducing small, manageable doses of discomfort into your day. This way, you gradually stretch your comfort zone, becoming more adaptable and better equipped to handle challenges. Here are some practical ways you can start right now:

1. Micro-Adventures

- Regularly engage in small but impactful adventures. Try a new hiking trail, camp overnight, explore a nearby town you've never visited, or simply pick a local spot on the map and explore. Each micro-adventure breaks your daily pattern and revitalizes your sense of curiosity and exploration.

147

2. Physical Challenges

Commit to regular physical stressors to build strength and resilience. Some ideas include:

(Always check with your doctor before starting these physical challenges.)

- **Cold Exposure:** Start your day with a cold shower or occasionally plunge into cold water (even if you have to work your way up to it, starting with just 15 seconds is great). This practice not only boosts mood and resilience but can also lower inflammation, improve circulation, and enhance metabolism.

- **Heat Exposure (Sauna Sessions):** Regular sauna use can significantly improve cardiovascular health, reduce inflammation, and enhance stress tolerance.

- **High-Intensity Exercise:** Regularly incorporate workouts that briefly push your physical limits, such as interval sprints, intense strength-training sessions, or vigorous circuit training. If you're older or new to exercise, choose activities that elevate your heart rate comfortably yet significantly, such as brisk uphill walking, faster-paced swimming, cycling, or even dancing. Aim for an intensity level where holding a conversation becomes challenging. Even short bursts of high-intensity training enhance cardiovascular health, strengthen muscles, boost metabolism, and stimulate beneficial hormonal responses, including increased growth hormone production. Remember, this controlled, temporary stress is beneficial: it builds physical resilience, improves overall fitness, and promotes longevity.

3. Mental Stretching

Challenge your brain regularly. Try activities that feel slightly intimidating at first:

- **Learn a New Skill:** Take up a foreign language, try coding, or learn a new sport or hobby. The initial difficulty strengthens your mental adaptability and confidence.

- **Creative Projects:** Start writing, painting, filming, or any other creative pursuit that initially feels outside your comfort zone. Each new skill develops your problem-solving ability and creativity.

4. Social Stretching

- Intentionally expand your social comfort zone. Consider joining a club or meetup group that aligns with your interests or even something entirely new to you. The first step might feel daunting, but connecting with new communities provides emotional support and enhances longevity through meaningful relationships.

5. Financial Challenges

Building financial resilience involves stepping into slightly uncomfortable territory:

- **Bitcoin Self-Custody:** Regularly withdraw your Bitcoin into your hardware wallet, learning the basics of secure self-custody and financial sovereignty.

- **Explore Bitcoin's Depth:** Bitcoin encompasses an incredibly diverse range of fields, including history, economics, game theory, computer science, psychology, energy, math, physics, networks, geopolitics, human rights, sociology, and finance. Personally, I've learned more from studying Bitcoin over the last four years than in all my formal education combined. Diving into Bitcoin goes beyond finances; it's an expansive intellectual adventure that sharpens your critical thinking, curiosity, and understanding of the world.

- **Dollar-Cost Averaging (DCA):** Commit to a steady, disciplined strategy of buying Bitcoin. This consistent practice builds financial discipline and reduces the emotional stress associated with market fluctuations.

6. Intentional New Experiences

Shake up routine tasks and deliberately introduce new experiences into everyday life:

- **Travel Differently:** Choose less predictable vacation spots, or try a completely new mode of travel, like a road trip, camping, or backpacking.

- **Change Daily Routines:** Occasionally vary your morning routine, meals, or routes to work. Small changes keep your brain engaged and alert.

Putting It All Together

Daily discomfort doesn't have to mean constant stress. It's about deliberately and consistently stepping beyond your familiar boundaries in controlled and intentional ways. Each small discomfort accumulates, building powerful physical, mental, emotional, and financial resilience. By incorporating these habits into your daily life, you're actively building strength today and resilience for tomorrow.

Grip Strength Recipe: A Powerful Longevity Tool

This might seem trivial, but research consistently shows that grip strength is one of the most reliable predictors of overall health and longevity. Developing strong grip strength is a practical way to directly build antifragility into your daily life. It actively enhances your resilience by reducing vulnerability to falls, fractures, and age-related decline, making you physically tougher and better equipped to thrive through life's inevitable stressors.

Why does grip strength matter so much?

- **Fall Prevention:** Strong grip strength enhances balance and stability, reducing the risk of falls, a leading cause of injury and disability in older adults.

- **Muscle Mass Indicator:** Grip strength reflects overall muscle mass and strength, which is crucial for maintaining mobility and independence as you age.

- **Bone Health:** There's a strong correlation between grip strength and bone mineral density, indicating stronger bones and reduced risk of osteoporosis.

- **Chronic Disease Risk:** Lower grip strength is linked with increased risks of heart disease, diabetes, and other chronic conditions.

- **Cognitive Function:** Studies indicate a connection between grip strength and cognitive health, with weaker grip strength associated with cognitive decline.

Ingredients:

- Pull-up bar (or sturdy overhead bar)

- Heavy weights (kettlebells, dumbbells, or heavy household objects)

- Hand grip trainer or stress ball

- Access to indoor/outdoor climbing wall (optional)

- Grip strength dynamometer (available online for around $25)

Instructions:

1. **Dead Hangs:**
   Hang from a pull-up bar for short periods, gradually increasing your duration over time. Regular dead hangs improve grip strength and support shoulder and spinal health.

2. **Farmer's Carry:**
   Walk short distances holding heavy weights in each hand. Gradually increase weight and distance to strengthen your grip, forearms, and core.

3. **Grip Trainers:**
   Squeeze hand grippers or stress balls daily, increasing repetitions or resistance as you get stronger. This provides incremental improvements in grip strength.

4. **Rock Climbing (optional but highly beneficial):**
   Regularly practice indoor or outdoor rock climbing to significantly challenge and enhance your grip and overall strength.

5. **Resistance Training:**
   Regularly incorporate exercises like deadlifts, rows, and pull-ups into your workouts to boost grip strength and overall muscular capacity.

6. **Regular Testing:**
   Periodically use your grip strength dynamometer to measure your progress. Adjust your routine accordingly to ensure continual improvement.

By focusing on grip strength, you're investing in an essential aspect of your overall health and longevity. Plus, you'll never again have to awkwardly ask someone to open that stubborn jar for you. You can be the hero.

Mindset Shift Recipe: Journaling & Learning Hour

Shifting your mindset toward growth and adaptability doesn't have to be complex or time-consuming. This recipe combines simple practices like intentional learning and brief daily journaling, both delivering powerful results.

Ingredients:

- Journal or notebook

- Pen

- One free hour each evening

- New topic, skill, or area of interest

Instructions:

1. Daily Journaling (5 minutes):

   - Each morning or evening, spend five minutes writing about challenges you've recently faced.

   - Actively reframe each challenge as an opportunity to learn and grow, rather than an obstacle.

   - Notice and reflect on how this small practice gradually shifts your stress response and mindset.

2. Nightly Learning Hour (1 hour):

   - Replace one hour of nightly TV or screen time with deliberate exploration.

   - Choose a topic completely outside your typical interests or professional expertise, such as history, philosophy, technology, or a new skill you've always wanted to explore.

   - After your learning session, briefly jot down a reflection or share your insights with someone. Reinforcing what you learn deepens your understanding and sustains curiosity.

This combined protocol builds a powerful habit loop: journaling fosters a growth-oriented mindset, and your nightly learning hour replaces passive consumption with active mental engagement, strengthening cognitive resilience and nurturing lifelong curiosity.

Part 3

Beyond Survival:
Thriving in the Era of Bitcoin, AI, and Longevity

Chapter 8

Entropy, Bitcoin & Longevity:
Fighting the Natural State of Decay

Entropy quietly shapes our lives, a subtle force lurking everywhere, gently pulling us toward chaos and disorder. Muscles weaken when left unused, cells age, and neglected systems inevitably crumble. I first understood entropy through my own body: untreated injuries, the fog from poor sleep, chronic inflammation that wouldn't fade. Ignored problems compound, transforming manageable issues into overwhelming crises.

Entropy may be inevitable, but it can be resisted.

When I started viewing Bitcoin and longevity as structured, intentional battles against entropy, everything changed. Both demand disciplined, intentional actions to counteract decay and preserve strength. This chapter explores how entropy affects our biology, finances, and minds, providing deliberate strategies to maintain clarity and vitality.

The Nature of Entropy

Entropy is best illustrated by sunlight. The sun continuously streams highly organized, low-entropy energy toward Earth. Plants capture this structured energy, converting it into usable forms that power life, creating complexity but also gradually increasing entropy. Ecosystems thrive, humans flourish, and complexity expands precisely because we harness this ordered energy. Without this constant flow of fresh energy from the sun, however, complexity rapidly collapses, and life inevitably drifts toward disorder and decay, toward maximum entropy.

157

Entropy, a fundamental law of thermodynamics, states that all systems naturally move toward chaos and deterioration. Bodies age. Structures deteriorate. Attention scatters. I often picture entropy like quicksand, probably because nearly every movie and show I watched as a kid had someone sinking helplessly into it, leaving my generation with a deeply ingrained, irrational fear. Like quicksand, entropy steadily pulls us down, yet we aren't entirely powerless. While sinking might be inevitable, we can control the rate at which it happens. The key lies in recognizing entropy's subtle yet pervasive grip and responding with deliberate, intentional actions to slow, or even temporarily reverse, the descent.

Biological Entropy: Protecting Your Health

Ignored inflammation → chronic pain
Subtle fatigue → constant exhaustion
Minor injuries → chronic injuries
Poor sleep → cognitive decline
Skipped workouts → muscle loss and frailty

This is biological entropy at work. Minor issues, overlooked, inevitably compound into serious health problems.

My first significant battle with entropy began with fasting. Initially skeptical, I soon learned that fasting triggers **autophagy**, our body's internal cleanup system. The results were subtle but profound: inflammation eased, energy levels rose, and mental clarity sharpened.

Sleep became equally crucial. Prioritizing deep sleep sharpens memory, strengthens the immune system, and reduces stress. Strength training added another layer of protection, improving mitochondrial function, boosting muscle mass, and turning fragility into resilience.

Managing my persistent back pain required a targeted approach: breathwork relieved muscle tension, strength training built spinal stability, and targeted red-light therapy accelerated cellular repair. These habits didn't permanently cure the issue, but they actively resisted entropy, keeping pain at bay through consistent vigilance and deliberate action.

Each healthy decision became intentional resistance:

- Sleep regenerates cells and reduces inflammation.

- Fasting clears cellular debris and supports metabolic health.

- Strength training boosts resilience and mitochondrial health.

- Nutrient-dense food nourishes and supports tissue repair.

Tracking these habits reinforced their importance, turning each action into deliberate resistance against biological entropy.

Mining Reward: Trigger Autophagy

Fasting flips on your body's internal clean up switch: autophagy. This powerful process ramps up during extended fasting, especially overnight, and breaks down damaged cells, clears debris, and supports regeneration.

Light activation begins around 12–16 hours of fasting, with moderate activation occurring around 24–48 hours. Eating before bed can stall autophagy by signaling to the body that nutrients are still available. Autophagy reduces inflammation, sharpens mental clarity, and may even eliminate precancerous cells. Think of it as your body's built-in longevity protocol, no prescription required.

Cellular Entropy: Mitochondria, Telomeres, and Longevity

Entropy becomes vividly apparent at the cellular level. As we age, telomeres, the protective caps on chromosomes, steadily shorten. Cells become older, lose their ability to regenerate properly, and start contributing to inflammation and aging. At the same time, mitochondrial function declines, reducing energy production and accelerating biological entropy.

Mitochondria, the tiny powerhouses inside your cells, rely on structured energy and clear biological signals for optimal performance. Natural sunlight, regular movement, and nutrient-dense foods keep mitochondria healthy and efficient. In contrast, disrupted circadian rhythms from irregular sleep or late-night screens impair mitochondrial function and accelerate cellular breakdown.

Melatonin is crucial for protecting mitochondria from oxidative stress, and its production depends directly on your daily exposure to natural light cycles. Without consistent signals from structured routines, melatonin levels drop, inflammation rises, and cellular entropy accelerates.

Emerging longevity therapies and biohacking techniques directly target cellular entropy. Practices like caloric restriction, intermittent fasting, NAD+ supplementation, hyperbaric oxygen therapy (HBOT), sauna sessions, cold exposure, and regular exercise can boost mitochondrial function, enhance cellular resilience, and promote telomere maintenance.

Every structured choice, including daily movement, disciplined sleep routines, controlled screen exposure, targeted supplements, and intentional beneficial stressors, actively defends against mitochondrial and cellular entropy. These deliberate habits help secure lasting vitality and resilience.

Environmental Entropy: Protecting Yourself from External Chaos

Environmental toxins, pollutants, and ultra-processed foods significantly accelerate biological entropy. During my travels in India, air pollution was so severe that it was equivalent to smoking thirteen cigarettes a day. Research indicates that prolonged exposure to polluted air can reduce life expectancy by approximately two years. Experiencing this firsthand emphasized the necessity of controlling air quality.

Today, my air purifier runs continuously, especially during wildfire season. I use an indoor air quality monitor to track PM2.5, fine particulate matter smaller than 2.5 microns that can penetrate deep into the lungs and enter the bloodstream. Breathing clean air helps support respiratory function, protect against chronic inflammation, and maintain overall cellular health.

I also regularly check outdoor air quality using reliable sources like IQAir. The World Health Organization recommends keeping annual average PM2.5 levels below 5 $\mu g/m^3$ due to the serious health risks associated with long-term exposure. Nearly 100 percent of the global population currently lives in areas exceeding this guideline. In response, the U.S. Environmental Protection Agency recently lowered its annual PM2.5 standard to 9 $\mu g/m^3$ to better protect public health. Monitoring these levels helps ensure both indoor and outdoor environments remain within safe limits.

To safeguard yourself from environmental entropy:

- Purify your air and water with reliable filtration systems. Reverse osmosis filtration works great for clean drinking water. For air purification, choose a filter specifically rated to remove PM2.5 particles.

- Minimize ultra-processed foods and prioritize whole, organic foods.

- Reduce plastic use, especially single-use plastics, to limit microplastic exposure and endocrine disruption.

- Spend more time outdoors in natural environments to reduce stress hormones, lower blood pressure, and enhance immune function.

Financial Entropy: The Inevitable Collapse of Fiat

Throughout history, fiat currencies inevitably spiral toward disorder and eventually collapse. Inflation erodes purchasing power, debts accumulate, and economies stumble into chaos. Humans simply cannot resist the temptation of the money printer, quietly diluting currency to fund wars, cover debts, or hide poor decisions, silently stealing wealth from their citizens.

As discussed in Chapter 4, this human mismanagement has deep historical roots. Ancient Rome famously clipped gold from coins, subtly increasing the money supply without mining more gold. In 1933, the U.S. government confiscated citizens' gold by force, then immediately devalued the dollar by changing gold's official price, effectively printing more money overnight. By 1971, the U.S. abandoned gold entirely, turning the dollar into pure fiat currency backed only by empty promises.

Across the globe, currency collapses echo this same pattern. Germany's Weimar Republic printed money so recklessly in the 1920s that paper bills became worthless overnight. Citizens burned currency to heat their homes because the bills had no value. More recently, Venezuela, Argentina, Brazil, Zimbabwe, Lebanon, Turkey, and Sudan endured severe hyperinflation, wiping out lifetimes of savings and plunging millions into poverty.

For much of my lifetime, the United States financed continuous wars through money printing rather than open taxation. Citizens would never voluntarily agree to fund these conflicts through increased taxes, as that would require accountability and transparency. Instead, governments choose stealth, silently extracting purchasing power from citizens through inflation.

Bitcoin disrupts this destructive pattern. Unlike fiat, Bitcoin's supply cannot be arbitrarily expanded. No government or individual can secretly dilute your wealth. Without unlimited access to the money printer, governments would require explicit citizen consent through transparent taxation before funding wars or irresponsible spending. Bitcoin replaces human weakness with math and code, rules instead of rulers. Whatever fiat currency you hold, whether dollars, euros, yen, or lira, its purchasing power inevitably fades. Protect your stored time and energy with something finite, something verifiable, something mathematically designed to resist entropy and maintain its structure over time.

Mining Entropy: Transforming Waste Energy into Bitcoin

Discovering Bitcoin mining showed me entropy management on a much larger scale. Bitcoin miners are mobile power consumers, serving as entropy fighters, chasing down wasted or stranded energy wherever it hides. At oil fields and landfills, they swap wasteful gas flaring for electric generators, converting methane into electricity. That electricity powers Bitcoin miners, transforming chaos into economic value.

Methane is no small threat. As a greenhouse gas in our atmosphere, methane traps 84 times more heat than CO_2 over a 20-year span and accounts for roughly 25% of global warming. Both oil wells and landfills are major contributors. In the U.S. alone, there are approximately 3,000 active landfills and 10,000 closed landfills, with over half leaking methane into the atmosphere. Traditional methane mitigation, such as flaring or converting methane to electricity, is expensive, poorly enforced, and imperfect. Even when flaring is implemented, up to 9% of methane still escapes into the atmosphere. Bitcoin miners using generators can capture and convert methane with up to 99.89% efficiency, significantly reducing emissions and transforming a climate liability into productive economic value.

In El Salvador, miners tap into previously unused and inaccessible geothermal energy from volcanoes and channel it into securing the Bitcoin network. Across the globe, energy that was once considered unusable is now being directed into a system that demands proof of work: verifiable effort, secured by natural law.

Bitcoin mining doesn't defy entropy; it works with it by channeling chaotic energy into something structured, scarce, and valuable. It's energy alchemy backed by math, physics, and incentives.

Mining Reward: Turn Polluted Air into Biological Wealth

Polluted air is chaotic and harmful, accelerating decay if left unchecked. Leaking methane from oil fields and landfills is a perfect example. Bitcoin miners combat this entropy by capturing harmful methane, converting it into electricity, and transforming waste into value. Similarly, your air purifier captures damaging particles before they enter your body, converting environmental disorder into clean, breathable air. By filtering what you inhale, you actively reclaim health from entropy.

Digital Entropy: From Noise to Clarity

Initially, the internet promised a new age of connection, open access, and limitless knowledge. But instead of clarity, it quickly descended into chaos, filled with misinformation, manipulated narratives, surveillance, and unreliable data. Digital entropy surged, creating confusion, division, and uncertainty at every click.

Bitcoin stands apart from this noisy digital landscape. While the broader online world struggles with truth distortion and data overload, Bitcoin offers mathematical certainty, transparency, and verifiable truth. Its immutable ledger ensures every transaction remains visible, permanent, and incorruptible, anchored in cryptographic proof rather than human trust.

In an era drowning in digital noise, Bitcoin's open, decentralized network provides economic stability and universal access. It restores order, offering a clear and unchanging source of truth, transforming digital entropy into structured clarity.

Informational Entropy: The Battle for Clarity

Today's digital landscape is a high-entropy battleground of endless scrolling, clickbait headlines, rapid-fire 10-second videos, and dopamine-driven "likes" that steadily erode our ability to focus, think deeply, and sustain curiosity. How can anyone, especially younger generations raised in this

163

environment, explore complex ideas or achieve true depth in a world that rewards shallow engagement?

Mainstream news media amplifies this entropy, leveraging propaganda and fearmongering to prey on emotions, keeping viewers triggered and addicted. Alarming headlines and anxiety-inducing narratives fuel cycles of superficial engagement and sustained mental chaos.

This relentless mental stimulation leads to informational entropy, an accelerating drift from clarity into chaos, from careful thinking into superficial distraction and cognitive decay.

What's the solution?

Intentional, independent education might be your best defense. Independent study, critical thinking, and lifelong curiosity build resilience, sharpening your ability to differentiate truth from noise. Instead of passively consuming content designed to hijack attention and stimulate quick dopamine hits, active learners ask questions, challenge narratives, verify facts, and embrace nuance.

Bitcoin's design protects against fiat entropy. Likewise, intentional learning protects against informational entropy. Books, podcasts, focused conversations, and independent study help maintain clarity and build resilience. Instead of passively scrolling, creating these structured habits harnesses dopamine intentionally, sharpening your mind and enabling you to distinguish truth from noise.

Independent thinking and lifelong curiosity are essential. Choosing depth over distraction preserves your ability to navigate an increasingly chaotic world.

Mining Reward: Read the White Paper

In a world drowning in misinformation, distraction, and digital noise, clarity is rare. The Bitcoin white paper is just nine pages, yet it changed everything. It's a masterpiece of order, logic, and elegant design. Try to read it in one sitting, with no phone, no tabs, no distractions. Reflect on how nine pages of precision created a new monetary universe. Entropy loves noise. The white paper is signal. Go back to the source. Clarity lives there. Read it here: bitcoin.org/bitcoin.pdf

Mental and Emotional Entropy

Entropy also erodes mental focus and emotional balance. Counteracting this mental chaos requires deliberate action:

- **Meditation** restores clarity.

- **Breathwork** eases anxiety.

- **Journaling** organizes thoughts.

- **Habit tracking** reinforces routines.

- **Gamifying workouts** redirects dopamine toward healthy behaviors.

These structured strategies help reclaim clear thinking and intentional living.

Entropy is relentless, inevitable, and all-consuming. But through intentional habits, disciplined strategies, and purposeful systems like Bitcoin, it can be actively resisted. Your actions today determine whether you succumb to disorder or build resilience, clarity, and a lasting foundation for tomorrow.

Cosmic Entropy: Bitcoin's Reflection of Universal Laws

Bitcoin mirrors the universe itself. In the beginning, the universe was impossibly dense, unimaginably concentrated, all energy tightly held within a single brilliant point. Then came the Big Bang, an explosion that sent energy racing outward, filling the emptiness with galaxies, stars, planets, and ultimately, life itself. Simple energy evolved into astonishing complexity, creating intricate structures and endless possibilities along the way.

Bitcoin's story started similarly: quiet, dense, and focused. It emerged from a single vision: the white paper, proposing a mathematically perfect form of digital money. At first, only visionaries, cypherpunks, and idealists saw its potential. Small clusters of early miners and curious enthusiasts exchanged this strange new digital asset almost experimentally. Gradually, through conversations and curiosity, the idea spread. People worldwide began recognizing the profound implications of money not controlled by any single entity, but governed purely by mathematics and code.

From its simple beginnings, Bitcoin expanded outward, creating vibrant ecosystems, new industries, and layers of innovation, from Lightning's instant transactions to censorship-resistant social media protocols like Nostr, open-source communities, and global adoption. Like stars emerging from cosmic dust, businesses, financial freedom, and economic empowerment blossomed, fueled by Bitcoin's expanding network.

The story of Bitcoin, much like the universe, continues unfolding. Just as the cosmos expands steadily, creating new worlds and opportunities, Bitcoin's potential continues to grow. Every node, miner, and user contributes energy to this expanding universe of economic possibility, transforming simplicity into ever-increasing complexity and empowerment.

On the other hand, Bitcoin behaves like a cosmic black hole, pulling distorted assets, like stocks, bonds, real estate, and gold, into its gravitational field, consolidating fragmented economic resources into structured order. Fiat currency distorts value, forcing people to store wealth in assets that inflate unnaturally because fiat itself cannot retain purchasing power. Like crossing the event horizon, the pull toward Bitcoin is inevitable: first gradually, then suddenly, all forms of stored value will surrender to its gravitational force.

Under a healthy monetary system, a house would simply be a home, a consumption good, not an investment vehicle used desperately to preserve purchasing power. Bitcoin fixes this distortion, perfecting money itself. Ultimately, Bitcoin will absorb the monetary premiums of all these assets as people shift their stored energy, effort, and time into a single, incorruptible financial core.

This balance between expansive growth and gravitational consolidation demonstrates Bitcoin's powerful resistance to entropy. Like the universe itself, Bitcoin is unstoppable. Every attempt to slow it down only makes it stronger, more resilient, and more inevitable.

The universe operates under strict, unwavering rules, laws of physics governing its very fabric. Bitcoin follows this cosmic precedent, defined not by human whims but by immutable mathematical laws. Its incorruptible ledger mirrors the universe's uncompromising adherence to rules, creating trust through predictability, neutrality, and transparency. Energy is the fundamental currency of the cosmos, endlessly transformed but never destroyed. Bitcoin embodies this universal principle, acting as humanity's universal battery. It captures, stores, and preserves the energy of our labor and creativity, safeguarding it against entropy and loss until precisely when it is needed.

Anti-Entropy Recipe: Mining for Heat

Energy is never truly wasted; it just needs direction. A Bitcoin miner draws electricity and produces heat. If you're already using electric heat, running a miner gives that same energy a second job: warming your space *and* earning sats while securing the network.

It's a practical way to battle entropy: reclaiming what would've been lost, putting it to work twice, and channeling waste into value. You're heating your home either way… why not get something in return?

Ingredients:

- ASIC miner (see my favorite recommendations below)

- Stable internet connection

- **Mining pool** account (Ocean, Braiins, Luxor etc.)

- Reliable power source (ideally electricity already used for heat)

- Proper housing or casing for noise and heat control (especially for larger units)

- Optional: Quiet cooling fans *(I recommend Noctua fans)*

Instructions:

1. **Choose your miner.**
   Here are two of my favorite plug-and-play options:

   - **Avalon Nano 3**
     Compact, beginner-friendly, quiet, and perfect as a desk-sized heater. Ideal for small rooms or offices.

   - **Urlacher by Altair Tech**
     More powerful, designed for larger spaces like entire rooms or homes. May require additional housing and noise control.

   - For more advanced home mining setups, check out altairtech.io or explore some of our home mining tutorials at youtube.com/@ 21millionfilms.

2. **Set up your mining space.**
   Depending on your chosen miner, consider soundproof housings and/ or quiet cooling fans *(Noctua fans work great)* to effectively manage

noise and heat. Ensure your space safely accommodates the generated heat.

3. **Connect your miner.**
   Plug into your power source and securely connect to the internet. Link your miner to your chosen mining pool *(Ocean, Braiins, etc.)*.

4. **Start mining.**
   Power on your miner and confirm successful hashing through your mining pool's dashboard.

5. **Maintain and optimize.**
   Monitor mining performance, temperature, and noise levels regularly. Adjust miner positioning and cooling as needed for optimal performance.

Benefits:

- Offset heating costs using electricity you're already paying for.

- Passively earn Bitcoin simply by heating your space.

- Strengthen decentralization by directly contributing hashing power to the Bitcoin network.

- Build practical, hands-on knowledge of Proof of Work and Bitcoin mining.

Mining for heat is a small way to reclaim control, turning wasted energy into value, and entropy into opportunity.

Chapter 9

The Intersection:
How AI and Bitcoin Will
Transform Health, Wealth, and Society

We're already witnessing the convergence of Bitcoin, AI, and longevity technologies. AI-powered wearables like Oura Ring, Whoop, and Apple Watch continuously track biometrics and transform raw data into actionable insights. Companies like Levels pair continuous glucose monitors with AI-driven analytics to optimize nutrition, reduce inflammation, and improve metabolic health. Apps like Don't Die let you import lab results and biological age tests, delivering personalized, actionable feedback to guide health decisions.

In Texas, Bitcoin miners stabilize power grids by automatically responding to real-time energy demands, absorbing excess electricity during low-use periods, and instantly powering down during shortages. Worldwide, Bitcoin mining finances renewable energy projects, turning previously stranded energy into meaningful economic growth.

In longevity research, labs like Altos Labs and Calico are actively targeting biological aging. Researchers have significantly extended lifespan in mice by manipulating genetic and epigenetic pathways, effectively "resetting" cells to a younger biological state. These advancements bring human longevity breakthroughs closer to reality.

Bitcoin is empowering the most financially vulnerable. Over a billion people worldwide are unbanked, with many others trapped using predatory financial services. Bitcoin lets them become their own bank, securely controlling their money without relying on traditional banks or facing oppressive financial regulations. Bitcoin is permissionless: anyone with an internet connection can store, send, and receive funds, no matter their location or financial situation.

AI & Personalized Medicine

AI is transforming healthcare from a reactive, symptom-driven system into proactive, personalized medicine. This shift empowers you with precise, data-driven insights, enabling early disease detection, proactive health optimization, and greater precision in decision-making.

Wearables aren't just counting steps anymore. Today, they continuously monitor biomarkers like heart rate variability, oxygen saturation, sleep patterns, and metabolic changes, detecting health issues like cardiovascular disease, diabetes, and neurological conditions long before symptoms appear. Devices like the Apple Watch perform electrocardiograms (EKGs), instantly alerting users to abnormal heart rhythms or potential cardiac events.

I've experienced this personally. My wearable signals subtle changes, such as spikes in wrist temperature or elevated heart rate, days before I notice symptoms from an illness, clearly marking when my body begins to struggle. Even minor choices, like eating late or drinking a single glass of wine, immediately affect my sleep and recovery. This instant feedback allows quick adjustments, significantly improving my health and resilience.

Biohacking, once considered niche, has become mainstream thanks to wearables and machine learning. Currently, around 34% of Americans regularly use wearable devices to track their health. Continuous biometric monitoring empowers people to understand their body's unique responses, optimizing their health through personalized insights.

Beyond wearables, deeper layers of data like full genome sequencing, microbiome analysis, blood biomarkers, and biological age assessments, now seamlessly integrate with and benefit from AI analysis. Athletes leverage these insights to refine recovery protocols, training loads, and nutrition strategies, boosting performance and reducing injury risk. Busy professionals optimize supplements, diets, sleep routines, and workouts based on their individual biology. As AI-driven recommendations become commonplace and testing costs continue to decline, relying on generic treatments and guesswork will soon seem outdated.

Traditional healthcare typically follows a reactive, one-size-fits-all approach: wait for symptoms, diagnose, then treat. Personalized medicine flips this model entirely. Instead of waiting, it pairs AI with real-time biometric and genetic data to proactively identify potential health issues and address their root causes.

AI is revolutionizing diagnostics, frequently surpassing human accuracy. Harvard's AI model CHIEF (Clinical Histopathology Imaging Evaluation Foundation) identified cancers such as esophageal, stomach, colon, and prostate tumors with nearly 94% accuracy. UCLA researchers developed an AI tool identifying prostate cancer with 84% accuracy, significantly outperforming human doctors at 67%. In breast cancer screening, AI reduced false positives by 37.3% and unnecessary biopsies by nearly 28%, maintaining high diagnostic accuracy. Another AI model from Daffodil International University achieved 99.26% accuracy in detecting endometrial cancer. As AI continues to refine diagnostics, detecting diseases long before symptoms emerge could soon become commonplace, shifting healthcare from uncertainty to early, accurate intervention.

AI's potential in everyday healthcare extends far beyond diagnostics. Wearables like the Apple Watch already demonstrate this by performing EKGs and instantly alerting users to irregular heart rhythms. AI also reshapes broader healthcare interactions, becoming integral to daily life. Apps like K Health analyze symptoms instantly, while mental health chatbots offer 24/7 emotional support, often rated as more empathetic and comprehensive than human doctors. According to studies from JAMA Internal Medicine, Google, and Harvard Health, users overwhelmingly preferred AI-generated responses, highlighting the limitations of rushed, profit-driven 15-minute medical appointments. AI fills this gap by providing patient, consistent, and accessible support, available whenever it's needed.

Just as I was finalizing this book, Microsoft unveiled its Medical AI Diagnostic Orchestrator (MAI-DxO). Tested on 304 complex clinical cases from the *New England Journal of Medicine*, it achieved roughly 85% accuracy, approximately four times higher than a panel of 21 experienced physicians who scored around 20%. MAI-DxO was not only more accurate but also reduced diagnostic costs by approximately 20%, thanks to smarter test selection.

This new approach to personalized healthcare empowers individuals and communities, creating greater autonomy over health outcomes. Personalized medicine is health sovereignty, giving you the tools to proactively protect and enhance your well-being. Just as Bitcoin gives you control over your wealth, personalized medicine gives you control over your health. With this power, you can approach the future with clarity, confidence, and optimism. After all, Bitcoin protects your time; longevity is what you do with it.

Mining Reward: Biological Uptime

UV radiation levels above 2 cause cellular damage, leading to inflammation, accelerated aging, and downtime for your body's internal network. Track daily UV levels easily through your weather app. Plan outdoor activities for early morning or late evening when UV exposure is minimal. During peak hours, use sunscreen and protective gear to keep your biological systems running smoothly.

Bitcoin: Financial Empowerment for the Most Vulnerable

Bitcoin is a tool of empowerment, transforming the lives of financially vulnerable people worldwide. Around 1.4 billion people globally remain unbanked, lacking essential financial services such as savings accounts and reliable money transfers. Even in developed countries like the U.S., millions are underbanked, pushed into predatory financial services like payday loans and check-cashing operations, disproportionately affecting the poorest communities.

Remittance payments represent another critical area where Bitcoin makes a significant impact. Traditional methods of sending money internationally often impose heavy fees, dramatically reducing the amount received by families who depend on these funds. Bitcoin enables instant, secure, and nearly free money transfers across borders, ensuring more money reaches the families who need it most.

Bitcoin directly addresses financial inequity by providing anyone with an internet connection and smartphone the ability to securely store, send, and receive money instantly, bypassing traditional banks and costly intermediaries. For women and refugees trapped in restrictive or dangerous situations, Bitcoin offers critical financial independence. Women in oppressive environments often lack the legal rights to open bank accounts or control their own money, making it extremely challenging to escape harmful and abusive circumstances. Similarly, refugees fleeing conflict often lose everything, and carrying physical currency exposes them to theft or confiscation by authorities or criminals. Bitcoin allows individuals in these vulnerable situations to securely control and transport their wealth by memorizing a simple 12-word recovery phrase, safeguarding their financial future against authoritarian seizure and corruption.

Activists operating under oppressive regimes also greatly benefit from Bitcoin. By providing a secure, censorship-resistant way of receiving and managing funds, Bitcoin allows activists to continue their essential work without fear of financial interference or confiscation.

By offering financial autonomy, security, and efficiency, Bitcoin fundamentally reshapes global economic dynamics. It empowers the most vulnerable, gives economic control back to individuals, and ultimately levels the playing field for everyone. Anyone can tap into and benefit from this open, global network.

Bitcoin as the Foundation for an AI Economy

Bitcoin's decentralized, neutral architecture makes it the ideal currency for AI-driven systems. The Lightning Network, enabling instant, nearly free microtransactions, is perfectly suited for streaming the low-value transactions required by AI. Autonomous vehicles could seamlessly pay for charging, parking, or tolls in Bitcoin, while AI-generated content could directly receive micropayments from consumers. Smart devices are already independently paying for data, energy, and digital services in Bitcoin thanks to the Lightning Network.

We're already seeing these use cases emerge in daily life: international remittance payments occur instantly through Lightning without high fees; platforms like Fountain Podcasts allow listeners to stream small Bitcoin payments ("streaming sats") directly to creators as they enjoy content; and social platforms like Nostr integrate Lightning, enabling users to effortlessly tip or "zap" each other for valuable insights or posts. Soon, online content paywalls could be frictionlessly unlocked with tiny Lightning payments, replacing clunky subscription models. Whether accessing articles behind paywalls or watching YouTube videos, users could easily reward creators directly, instantly tipping for quality content.

As AI and Bitcoin increasingly overlap, understanding Bitcoin basics, such as self-custody, Lightning transactions, and running your own node, positions you to thrive in this rapidly evolving landscape. AI, like Bitcoin, is a powerful tool. When used intentionally, it can significantly amplify your health, financial independence, and productivity. Embrace AI proactively, letting it empower and elevate your life.

Game Theory: Why Early Adopters Always Win

History consistently rewards those who embrace new technologies first, often in the face of skepticism or outright dismissal.

When the telephone first arrived, Western Union scoffed:

> "This 'telephone' has too many shortcomings
> to be seriously considered as a means of
> communication."

(Internal memo, Western Union, 1876)

Ironically, Western Union again finds itself on the wrong side of history. Today, it operates as an overpriced remittance company, increasingly obsolete in the face of Bitcoin's instant and nearly free global transactions.

When automobiles emerged, a banker told Henry Ford's lawyer:

> "The horse is here to stay, but the automobile is
> only a novelty—a fad."

(Horace Rackham's banker, 1903)

Even electricity faced skepticism:

> "When the Paris Exhibition closes, electric light
> will close with it, and no more will be heard of it."

(Oxford professor Erasmus Wilson, 1878)

Television, too, was initially dismissed:

> "Television won't be able to hold on to any market
> it captures after the first six months. People will
> soon get tired of staring at a plywood box every
> night."

(Darryl F. Zanuck, Head of 20th Century-Fox, 1946)

Skepticism surrounded human flight as well:

> "Man won't fly for a million years."

(Editorial, New York Times, 1903)

This headline was published just days before the Wright brothers' historic first flight, demonstrating how quickly human ingenuity can overturn even the strongest doubts.

And when the internet began taking hold, many dismissed its staying power:

> "I predict the Internet will soon go spectacularly
> supernova and in 1996 catastrophically collapse."

(Robert Metcalfe, Inventor of Ethernet, 1995)

In 1997, acknowledging his mistake, Metcalfe famously blended a printed copy of this prediction with liquid and drank the mixture on stage.

Even as late as 2000, some newspapers remained skeptical:

"The internet may just be a passing fad as millions
give up on it."

(Daily Mail, 2000)

Yet, soldiers who adopted firearms reshaped nations. Businesses that leveraged email surged past competitors reliant on traditional mail. People who embraced automobiles quickly outpaced those clinging to horses. History repeatedly rewards those who embrace change early and decisively.

Today, we see this clearly with Bitcoin. Early adopters enjoy significant financial freedom compared to those who hesitate or remain skeptical. Each passing year widens this gap, rewarding those who recognized Bitcoin's potential early.

And it's still early.

BitcoinDeaths.com tracks every instance Bitcoin has been declared "dead" by supposed "experts" and the media. At the time of writing, Bitcoin has already "died" 430 times.

This skepticism toward innovation is deeply embedded in human nature, and health is no exception. When AI first started transforming healthcare, fear-driven headlines quickly emerged, warning about robots replacing doctors, privacy invasions from wearable devices, and misdiagnoses caused by AI-driven diagnostics. Not to mention the Hollywood movies portraying robots and AI uprisings. Just as with past technological advancements, these fears tend to overshadow the enormous potential benefits. The decisions you make today shape your quality of life decades from now. You can replace guesswork with precision and personalized strategies by embracing AI, using wearables and data-driven insights, staying current with emerging health research, and proactively refining your habits. Embrace technology for better health and a better life.

WHOOP, the wearable company, recently analyzed 4.3 million nights of objective sleep data collected from nearly 15,000 participants, not estimates or self-reported surveys, but actual, measurable biometric information. Their analysis provided clear, actionable insights. For instance, they found that strenuous evening workouts disrupt sleep unless completed at least four hours before bedtime. Early adopters of this technology immediately benefited from personalized, data-driven guidance, while the broader public gained practical, evidence-based strategies to significantly improve their sleep quality.

Earning my Personal Trainer certification in early 2025 revealed just how quickly conventional methods fall behind. Nutrition guidelines, exercise techniques, and even basic skills like measuring blood pressure felt years out of date. Similarly, in college, professors trained us on outdated cameras and methods, leaving us unprepared for emerging digital trends. My first job as a web video producer didn't exist when I started college, or even two years before graduation. Given this rapid pace of change, how can students confidently choose majors when we can barely predict the skills they'll need in six months? Academia often prepares students perfectly for yesterday, rarely for tomorrow.

But education itself is now evolving rapidly. AI-driven platforms will soon connect learners everywhere to the world's best teachers. Geography and institutional gatekeepers won't limit access to knowledge anymore. Want to learn physics from a Nobel laureate or philosophy from a renowned thinker? AI-powered education will soon make this reality accessible to everyone. The best teachers will reach students worldwide, delivering personalized curriculums tailored to each learner's unique strengths and interests.

Yet even when powerful tools like these are available, fear and inertia often hold us back. After multiple heart attacks and strokes, my grandma became trapped by chronic pain, immobilized by her fear of falling again or returning to the hospital. Staying still felt safer than risking further setbacks. But a gentle push from her physical therapist to try some basic exercises helped her see a new path forward. Similarly, AI can provide that gentle encouragement, like a personal trainer or therapist offering regular check-ins, consistent motivation, and personalized guidance with infinite patience. In today's world, knowledge is power, and that power is increasingly available to anyone with an internet connection. By embracing technology and proactively adapting, you actively shape your future instead of passively reacting to change. In a rapidly evolving world, adaptability quickly becomes your most critical skill.

You don't have to stay stuck when the knowledge you need is right at your fingertips. You have the power to improve your life.

Staying Ahead in an Accelerating World

The pace of technological change is exponential. The shifts we'll experience in the next decade may reshape our lives more profoundly than the past thousand years combined. Imagine traveling back just 100 years and trying to explain the internet, instant global communication, seeing faces across continents, unlimited information access, and instantly streaming any movie, song, or artwork. Today, we barely notice this everyday magic.

AI, Bitcoin, personalized medicine, and automation arrive faster each day, with greater impact. Staying ahead means actively embracing change and continuously exploring new ideas. Building resilience through lifelong learning and adaptability is crucial. Instead of fearing the unknown, choose curiosity and actively engage with emerging technologies.

Your future depends on your ability to embrace and adapt to the accelerating pace of change.

> "Our passion for learning ... is our tool for survival."
>
> - Carl Sagan

Adapt or Die

In 1962, President John F. Kennedy stood before a large crowd at Rice University and laid out a challenge that seemed nearly impossible at the time: landing a man on the moon within the decade. Kennedy openly embraced the difficulty, famously stating, "We choose to go to the moon... not because it is easy, but because it is hard."

Tackling seemingly impossible challenges often leads to breakthroughs we never anticipated. Kennedy's moonshot spurred innovations far beyond space travel itself, influencing computing, communication, and countless technologies still central to our lives today.

Now, we face our own moonshot moment. AI, Bitcoin, and personalized medicine are rapidly transforming our world, reshaping the ways we manage health, finances, and our collective futures. Early adopters of Bitcoin have unlocked greater financial independence, while those embracing AI-driven healthcare gain powerful insights that measurably improve their lives.

Yet embracing these technologies requires acknowledging our own biological limitations. Humans stopped evolving biologically too soon. Our ancient brains still crave sugar, fat, and instant gratification because calorie-dense foods once meant survival. Back then, sugary berries, fatty nuts, and calorie-rich meats provided essential fuel for survival. But today, our brains can't tell the difference between those healthy ancestral foods and modern ultra-processed snacks loaded with refined sugars and unhealthy fats. This mismatch causes cravings and hunger signals that frequently mislead us. What I'm saying is: you can't always trust your brain, it doesn't always act in your best interest. Our evolutionary wiring no longer aligns with our modern environment.

Here's where AI-driven automation steps in. Instead of relying on emotional or instinctive decisions, you can leverage AI and data-driven insights to optimize your body, mind, and life. Personalized AI algorithms can precisely determine what, when, and how much you should eat, removing guesswork and unhealthy impulses. AI can suggest optimal timing for supplements, create tailored workout schedules, structure daily movements, and even fine-tune your sleep protocol.

This doesn't mean giving up your free will to technology. Instead, you're building a personal system grounded in data and automation. Proactively structuring your environment and daily routines helps you consistently choose what's genuinely good for you, rather than what your outdated biology instinctively desires. With these new tools available, why wouldn't you give yourself every advantage to operate at your highest potential?

History consistently rewards those who proactively engage with change. Kennedy's ambitious goal was not only about reaching the moon. It was about embracing uncertainty to shape a better future. Today, we face a similar choice. Approaching rapid technological change with courage, curiosity, and adaptability ensures we don't just survive but thrive in this evolving landscape. By embracing AI and innovation, you can leverage technology to overcome outdated biological impulses, optimize your decisions, and actively shape a better future.

The Erosion of Problem-Solving Skills

We now live in a completely different world than the one our brains evolved to handle. Rapid technological advancement fundamentally reshapes how we think, communicate, and connect. Our ancestors navigated simpler environments, relying on careful observation, deep thinking, and face-to-face interaction. Today, we're inundated with instant information and continuous digital stimulation, challenging our ability to maintain meaningful relationships and adapt effectively to constant change. Strengthening these essential human skills has never been more important for navigating the complexity of modern life.

As technology accelerates, our relationship to information changes significantly. With instant access to productive answers and misinformation alike, our motivation to deeply analyze problems diminishes. This instant gratification weakens our critical thinking skills, gradually reducing our capacity to thoughtfully evaluate what's accurate and true.

This shift partly explains why conspiracy theories and anti-intellectualism are thriving. For some, believing in simplified or contrarian explanations delivers a quick dopamine hit. It feels good to think you have special insights that others don't. It feels empowering to question what "experts" say, even when those experts base their findings on careful research. It's an emotional reward rather than a logical choice. Questions or statements like "Do you really believe we landed on the moon?" or "Nobody actually died from COVID" aren't about evidence. They're about a sense of superiority or control in a complex world.

Narratives and Pattern Recognition

Humans have always been drawn to simplified narratives. Historically, pattern recognition helped us survive. We predicted seasons, navigated by the stars, and spotted danger early. But this skill also works against us when we perceive patterns where none exist. Our brains sometimes seek comfort by creating stories that offer a false sense of control over the unknown.

When people struggle to fully grasp complex realities, simplifying them can feel reassuring. This is how modern-day flat Earth theories or elaborate conspiracies gain traction; they offer certainty in an uncertain world. Many believers in these theories also hold strong religious views, reconciling these beliefs by rejecting mainstream scientific explanations. Believing in a flat Earth or staged events makes reality feel manageable and predictable, even when the truth is far more complex.

Our current political landscape reflects this as well. Politicians often create simplified narratives that appeal to emotions rather than being based on facts. These stories resonate because complexity can be exhausting. Few people take the time to critically evaluate what's presented, allowing group-think to take hold. Truth becomes secondary to the comfort of belonging or emotional satisfaction.

Admittedly, writing this book makes me wonder if I'm just seeing patterns everywhere, connecting dots between Bitcoin, longevity, and my own life. But hey, maybe that's exactly what helps us navigate complexity.

Community, Longevity, and Blue Zones

As mentioned previously, Blue Zones offer powerful insights into navigating rapid change. These are areas where people consistently live longer, healthier lives, partly due to strong community ties, mutual support, and a clear sense of purpose. Community serves as a powerful buffer against uncertainty. Whether in Japan, Italy, or Costa Rica, the common factor is clear: people face challenges collectively, never alone.

For instance, in Okinawa, residents form social circles called *moais*, small groups that meet regularly for mutual emotional support and financial assistance, often lasting decades or even lifetimes. In Costa Rica's Nicoya Peninsula, multi-generational households ensure older family members remain actively engaged and valued contributors, preserving their sense of purpose. Sardinian villages regularly gather around communal activities and celebrations, reinforcing their cultural bonds and mutual reliance.

When communities unite around shared goals, resilience naturally follows. In our rapidly changing technological landscape, such interconnectedness is essential. The collective wisdom and cultural traditions found in Blue Zones illustrate how facing challenges as a community strengthens adaptability. People don't navigate shifts alone; they discuss, deliberate, learn from each other, and collectively embrace solutions.

During the pandemic, I experienced firsthand how powerful online community-building could be. Platforms like Clubhouse, an audio-based social app, allowed me to form connections with Bitcoiners around the globe. As I mentioned earlier, communities like Plebnet emerged directly from platforms like Telegram and Clubhouse, thriving on shared experimentation and collaboration. Online spaces such as these make it easier than ever to find your tribe, to connect, learn, and build around shared interests or goals. Even when physical gatherings were impossible, these digital communities proved that technology, intentionally designed around meaningful interactions, can strengthen human connections rather than isolate us.

How can we cultivate similar communities? It begins by deliberately creating spaces for connection and dialogue, whether local meetups, regular social gatherings, or shared online platforms dedicated to mutual support. It involves actively preserving the wisdom of elders, encouraging cross-generational interactions, and creating tangible opportunities for meaningful, purpose-driven collaboration.

Moreover, the Blue Zone model can inspire us to rethink our approach to technology itself, prioritizing tools that enhance genuine human interaction rather than isolate us. Whether through decentralized social platforms like Nostr, open-source educational communities, or technologies explicitly designed for community building, we can intentionally foster stronger connections, shared resilience, and a clear sense of collective purpose. Choosing to actively engage with or even create these types of communities can profoundly influence individual longevity as well as the overall health and resilience of society.

The remarkable adaptability and collective strength seen in Blue Zones remind us that the path toward longevity, health, and thriving communities lies in facing change together. Harnessing the power of community, shared values, and mutual support equips us to confidently navigate technological shifts and proactively shape a healthier, more connected future.

The Need for a Shared Future Vision

To successfully navigate the accelerating pace of technological change, we need clear, compelling visions that unite us around shared goals. Articulating long-term aspirations, like Kennedy's moonshot, can inspire innovation, resilience, and a deeper, collective engagement with complex challenges.

When JFK challenged America to reach the moon, his vision inspired innovation, resilience, and unity. That ambitious goal energized an entire nation, sparking technological advancements and bringing people together to achieve something extraordinary.

Today, articulating similar long-term visions feels challenging. Short-term thinking often dominates our politics, economics, and everyday interactions, driven by immediate rewards, impulsive decisions, and "YOLO" attitudes. This short-sighted approach limits our collective ability to thoughtfully shape the future.

Yet we now have a chance to shift toward something more substantial. AI, Bitcoin, and personalized medicine represent collective opportunities, not just individual ones. Proactively embracing these technologies can unify us around meaningful goals, much like Kennedy's moonshot did decades ago. While embracing complexity may initially feel overwhelming, it enables us to make better decisions and build stronger, more resilient systems. For instance, understanding how Bitcoin works can seem daunting at first due to its technical nature. However, taking the time to grasp its principles can lead to greater financial independence and resilience against economic uncertainty. When we engage deeply with complex ideas rather than avoiding them, we equip ourselves to handle rapid change more effectively.

So, what will our moonshot be? Abundance for all? Clean, limitless energy and nutritious food? Colonizing distant planets? Solving aging and eliminating disease?

We stand at the edge of possibility, limited only by our imagination and courage. The future is ours to shape…what an exciting time to be alive.

Continuous Learning Recipe

The best preparation for an uncertain future is continuous learning. Actively seek reliable sources, thoughtfully explore complex topics, and approach new ideas with curiosity instead of judgment. AI can support this, providing personalized insights, learning pathways, and ongoing feedback. Use AI to remain updated, challenge assumptions, and refine your understanding of the rapidly evolving world.

Ingredients:

- Online learning platforms (e.g., Coursera, Khan Academy, Codecademy, Brilliant)

- Books, audiobooks, or podcasts

- Personalized AI-driven learning tools or apps

- Daily time commitment (aim for at least 1 hour)

Instructions

1. Set aside at least one hour each day dedicated to learning: consider replacing an hour of TV with focused learning.

2. Select a topic that aligns with your interests or professional goals.

3. Sign up for a course online, explore new topics through books, audiobooks, or podcasts, or use a personalized AI-driven learning app.

4. Engage actively: read or listen attentively, take notes, and summarize key points to reinforce retention.

5. Use AI-powered learning tools to track your progress, identify topics for deeper exploration, and recommend complementary content based on your learning patterns.

Local Business Bitcoin Integration Recipe

Just as Blue Zones teach us the power of community ties and shared purpose in fostering health and resilience, supporting local businesses through Bitcoin payments can strengthen your community's economic health and connectedness. This actionable recipe helps you engage locally, enhance financial literacy, and cultivate the collective strength and adaptability that make Blue Zones thrive.

Ingredients:

- A local business you support

- Bitcoin payment solutions (BTCPay Server, Strike, OpenNode)

- Educational resources on Bitcoin and Lightning Network

Instructions:

1. Approach a local business and express your interest in supporting them with Bitcoin payments.

2. Provide easy-to-understand resources highlighting Bitcoin's advantages: instant settlement and extremely low fees compared to traditional credit cards (typically 3%).

3. Help the business set up a Bitcoin payment solution like BTCPay Server or Strike.

4. Demonstrate the process by making your first purchase using Bitcoin.

5. Encourage the business to display visible Bitcoin signage or QR codes to attract additional customers and foster local economic resilience.

6. Regularly support and promote businesses adopting Bitcoin to strengthen community ties and local economies.

Chapter 10

Future-Proofing Your Life:
The Blueprint for Navigating Change

This book has explored how Bitcoin, longevity, and proactive health strategies can transform your future. But understanding is only half the battle; taking intentional action is what truly makes the difference.

Entropy is relentless, constantly pushing us toward disorder, decay, and chaos. Resisting it requires deliberate actions, clear strategies, and consistent routines. Throughout this book, I've shared personal stories highlighting strategies and tools I use daily to stay physically strong, mentally sharp, and financially secure.

This final chapter provides a practical blueprint, summarizing key strategies you've already encountered and introducing several new tools and ideas to help you future-proof your life. Consider this your personal playbook; it's filled with concrete steps for navigating uncertainty, optimizing health, building physical and financial resilience, and embracing change with clarity and purpose.

Preparing for the Unpredictable

No one truly knows what the future holds, but one thing is clear: we are entering an era unlike any other. We stand at the threshold of superintelligence, a world where technology and artificial intelligence promise to transcend limitations previously thought insurmountable. Things that were once purely in the realm of science fiction might soon become everyday realities. Diseases could be cured, abundance could become the norm, visiting other planets or even exploring distant solar systems could be within our reach, and life in general might become significantly easier and more fulfilling.

Yet this promising future brings its own set of challenges. The pace of change will accelerate faster than anything we've experienced, potentially making much of what we know today obsolete. Approaching this new world will require adaptability, openness, and a willingness to continually learn. Most importantly, it will require genuine human connection, taking the time to help others navigate these changes and sharing what you've learned.

To be ready for whatever the future holds, you first need to make sure you're actually here to experience it. Proactive wellness, taking care of yourself physically and mentally, is the foundation for adaptability and resilience.

Effectively navigating this uncharted territory also requires cultivating a beginner's mind, continually open to new information and ready to discard outdated beliefs. Intentionally surround yourself with people who elevate your thinking and challenge your perspectives, fostering continuous growth and development. Regularly dedicate time to reflection and recalibration of your goals. Question everything, even your deepest assumptions. By embracing uncertainty with curiosity and a proactive mindset, you position yourself to adapt and thrive in any future scenario.

One of the most powerful aspects of Bitcoin and longevity is their ability to unite people across diverse, often contradictory groups. Different ages, socioeconomic backgrounds, and philosophies rarely converge, but the shared desire for healthier bodies and sounder money changes that. The future built around Bitcoin and longevity isn't isolated or elitist. It's collaborative, inclusive, and widely accessible, creating a vision everyone can support.

Harnessing the Power of Simple Reminders

For years, I thought meaningful change depended solely on willpower. But willpower is limited. It often left me drained, inconsistent, and frustrated. Real, lasting change began when I discovered the simple yet powerful strategy of automated reminders.

Modern life is increasingly sedentary, dominated by hours spent sitting at desks, commuting, or relaxing on couches. Recent studies suggest that sitting too much may be nearly as harmful to our health as smoking, significantly increasing risks of cardiovascular disease, diabetes, and even premature death. Research from the Aerobics Center Longitudinal Study found that men sitting more than 23 hours per week had a 64% higher risk of cardiovascular death compared to those sitting fewer than 11 hours per week.

Sometimes we just need to move. Our ancestors led dramatically different lives; studies of traditional societies like the Hadza, Tsimane, and Amish report average daily step counts ranging from 14,000 to 18,000 steps, or roughly eight miles, as part of routine survival and daily activity. Realizing how drastically my own lifestyle had drifted from that, I decided to try setting hourly movement reminders. My smartwatch gently prompts me each hour to stand, stretch, or take a short walk. At first, I wasn't convinced it would help much. But within a week, these subtle nudges noticeably boosted my energy levels and productivity.

Mining Reward: Standing Desk & Walking Pad

Upgrade your workspace to take hourly movement a step further. Consider a standing desk and an under-desk walking pad. These tools seamlessly integrate movement into your day, keeping your energy high, metabolism active, and productivity consistently elevated.

Nutrition is another area where automated reminders have significantly improved my daily routine. I started using a fasting app that clearly signals when to begin and end my eating window, helping me control my caloric intake and reduce late-night snacking. On days when I'm not using the app but still want to optimize sleep, I'll set a separate reminder for my last meal of the day, usually around five to six hours before bedtime. This simple adjustment has made a surprising difference; I noticed dramatically better sleep quality, fewer digestion issues, and greater overall consistency in my meal timing.

I also set daily hydration nudges, reminding me periodically to stay properly hydrated. This practice, though seemingly minor, noticeably reduced my afternoon fatigue and improved my mental clarity and focus.

Mental health reminders can also be incredibly valuable. While I personally tend to find calm by regularly walking, particularly in nature (which we'll explore further later in this chapter), brief mindfulness check-ins throughout the day can help significantly reduce stress and boost emotional resilience. Even simple alerts prompting you to pause, breathe deeply, or step outside briefly can have powerful effects. Although these quick mindfulness breaks aren't currently part of my routine, they're a practice I highly recommend trying, especially if finding larger blocks of calm in your day is challenging.

Finally, personalized goal reminders tailored to specific aspirations, such as taking supplements, reviewing biometric data, or dedicating time to meaningful relationships, help me stay intentional and focused. I've also found AI helpful for creating personalized schedules and plans, including supplement timing, workout routines, and even recipe ideas. Additionally, my husband and I have a scheduled reminder each Sunday for our weekly check-in, where we discuss our upcoming plans, goals, and hopes for the week ahead. Completing these tasks provides immediate positive reinforcement, creating small dopamine hits that further encourage consistency and progress.

The strength of simple reminders is how effortlessly they fit into daily life. In a world full of distractions, automated nudges quietly guide me toward intentional routines aligned with my long-term health and personal goals. Over time, these habits become ingrained, reducing the need for reminders until they're eventually unnecessary.

Building Financial Resilience and Sovereignty

Financial resilience doesn't require wealth to start. I learned this firsthand, starting from essentially nothing. During my internship with Miss Universe, we spent a month in Las Vegas covering the Miss USA pageant. Surrounded by glamour, luxury hotels, and perfectly presented pageant contestants, my own reality was very different. I was broke. The contestants, focused on staying thin, rarely ate much, so each day I'd discreetly swipe leftover food from their trays to stay fed. Glamorous? Hardly. But it was practical, resourceful, and kept me going.

When I later moved to California, money remained extremely tight. I took full advantage of every free food offering at work: donuts, pastries, and bagels. None of it was particularly nutritious, but at least it was free. Living paycheck to paycheck, I quickly learned how fragile financial security could be. At any moment, an unexpected expense could derail everything. It was a stressful cycle I desperately wanted to break.

Then I discovered Bitcoin, and things started to change. Initially, Bitcoin felt abstract and overly complex. But I soon realized something essential: it's hard to truly understand Bitcoin until you own some yourself. Lightning didn't fully make sense to me until I ran a Lightning node. Mining felt purely theoretical until I started mining. Self-custody seemed complicated until I took full control of my own Bitcoin. Bitcoin is experiential, something you must do to truly grasp.

Starting small, I began setting aside tiny amounts of money to buy Bitcoin each month. Over time, that simple act evolved into real financial discipline. For the first time, I felt optimistic about my financial future. Watching my Bitcoin holdings slowly grow, independent of banks or inflationary policies, was profoundly empowering.

Holding Bitcoin offers a clear alternative to relying solely on traditional fiat currency. Rather than trusting governments or banks to maintain the value of your savings, Bitcoin gives you control over your own financial stability. Likewise, choosing privacy-focused tools like Nostr, a decentralized alternative to traditional social media, allows you to consciously support technologies that respect your freedom and autonomy. It's about making intentional choices, deciding whether you're contributing to outdated systems or actively building better ones.

If you're interested in developing your own financial resilience, my advice is straightforward: buy a small amount of Bitcoin. You don't need much to start. Right now, you can get roughly 1,000 sats for just $1. (I'm including this in the book to look back on and remember how cheap Bitcoin was.) Just get some and experience how it works. Learn about it by using it. Set up a weekly buy to automate your savings. To help you on this journey, check out resources on my site, **erinemalone.com**, where I've curated books, podcasts, videos, and hardware recommendations designed to guide you from beginner to confident Bitcoiner.

Financial resilience begins with a mindset shift, a willingness to learn, and consistent small actions. Bitcoin taught me that even starting from essentially nothing, you can steadily build financial autonomy and lasting security. If I can do it, so can you.

Mining Reward: Family Multi-sig

In Bitcoin, a multisig wallet requires multiple signatures to secure funds. Your family's future works the same way. Every member plays a role in securing long-term health and prosperity. Lead by example, build strong habits together, and share what you've learned to secure your family's future.

Enhancing Human Potential with Tech

Technology has fundamentally reshaped my approach to health and wellness. Rather than guessing how my body feels or blindly following general health advice, advanced tracking tools have allowed me to pinpoint exactly what I need to optimize. From daily biometrics to comprehensive biological tests, these technologies have transformed vague goals into precise targets.

My Apple Watch, for example, has evolved into my daily health companion. Throughout this book, I've shared how tracking metrics like resting heart rate (RHR), heart rate zones, heart rate variability (HRV), and VO$_2$ max has provided clear benchmarks for improvement. Instead of casually monitoring these numbers, I actively treat them like scores in a game, consistently aiming to set new personal bests. Every workout becomes a chance to beat my previous performance, driving both motivation and tangible improvements in my health.

Yet among all the metrics I've tracked, sleep has proven to be the most transformative. I didn't realize how much poor sleep impacted me until I began consistently monitoring and optimizing it. Using detailed sleep tracking, I discovered patterns and habits that significantly affected my recovery, mood, cognitive clarity, and overall health. Once I prioritized consistent, quality sleep, everything changed. Suddenly, my energy levels soared, brain fog vanished, and I felt more resilient physically and mentally. It's hard to grasp how poorly you're functioning until you've experienced the profound shift brought on by consistently good sleep.

Beyond daily metrics, deeper analyses like comprehensive blood panels and biological age tests have become integral to my health strategy. Every six months, I conduct a biological age test through TruDiagnostic, providing insights into my cellular health and aging rate. By pairing this information with regular blood panels and having AI analyze all my health data, I can precisely fine-tune my supplements, workouts, and overall lifestyle. AI simplifies what would otherwise be overwhelming, turning pages of raw data into actionable advice tailored specifically to my biology.

In addition to these tests, other proactive health screenings are worth considering, such as regular DEXA scans for assessing body composition, glucose monitoring for metabolic health, and periodic MRI screenings. These tests provide deeper insights into your body's current state and future risks. As technology advances and becomes increasingly affordable, incorporating these screenings can further refine your nutrition, supplementation, and training protocols.

I believe we're moving rapidly toward a future where each person will have their own personalized AI health assistant. This AI will continuously monitor, analyze, and optimize our routines, taking the guesswork entirely out of proactive health management. While some might choose to opt out, this seems increasingly unlikely to me. It's part of that "adapt or die" reality; perhaps quite literally. Why would anyone choose to forego technology that clearly improves health, performance, and quality of life?

Embracing these tools today is about much more than convenience or efficiency. It's about unlocking your full human potential. We already have the technology to proactively shape our health trajectories, detect problems long before symptoms appear, enhance longevity, and significantly improve our daily well-being. To me, there's no compelling reason to opt out of feeling better, performing at your best, and truly thriving.

Resetting Your Mind and Nervous System

Imagine a time when humans lived deeply connected to the natural world, guided by the rhythms of sunrise and sunset. Darkness was complete and unbroken, allowing uninterrupted rest. Silence, occasionally punctuated by the distant howl of a wolf or rustling leaves, provided true mental clarity. Life unfolded at a pace dictated by the seasons, free from constant notifications or digital alerts.

Today, our reality couldn't be more different. From the moment we open our eyes, we're swept into a digital whirlwind. Phones buzz constantly, emails flood our inboxes, social media demands immediate attention, and endless streams of information compete for our focus. Our nervous systems, never designed for such constant stimulation, remain locked in perpetual fight-or-flight mode, creating cycles of dopamine hits, chronic stress, anxiety, and mental fatigue.

Beyond digital distractions, modern life surrounds us with persistent background noise from airplanes, traffic, construction, and machinery. Studies show that for every 10-decibel increase in background noise, rates of anxiety medication use and stress-related conditions rise significantly. Our nervous systems struggle to cope with this constant sensory overload, leaving us chronically on edge.

Tools designed to help us, like the simple reminders I previously recommended, can unintentionally add to this noise if not managed carefully. While these reminders provide structure and consistency, they also highlight the importance of clear boundaries. Setting aside dedicated digital detox periods each day, even briefly, helps us reclaim balance and find relief from overstimulation.

I know firsthand how overwhelming this endless stimulation can become. At times, it feels like every waking moment there's something demanding immediate attention. Silence can seem foreign, boredom nearly nonexistent. I've caught myself reflexively reaching for my phone during moments meant for rest or reflection. This realization led me to seek change.

To reset and restore balance, I've consciously prioritized reconnecting with nature. One practice I've found especially powerful is the Japanese tradition called **Shinrin-Yoku**, or forest bathing. Forest bathing involves deliberately immersing yourself in nature, fully experiencing the quiet, scents, and subtle details around you. Researchers studying this practice discovered that participants who spent mindful time in forests experienced measurable reductions in stress hormones like cortisol and adrenaline, lowered blood pressure, and enhanced immune function. These positive effects persisted for days afterward, demonstrating that even brief retreats into nature can profoundly heal our overstimulated minds.

Further studies have shown that regularly spending time in forests actively boosts the body's defenses against illness. Trees naturally release substances called phytoncides, which increase the activity of natural killer (NK) cells, a vital part of our immune response. A 2023 study from Japan found that individuals living in regions with greater forest coverage experienced significantly lower mortality rates from cancers, including lung, breast, prostate, kidney, and colon cancers.

However, simply being in nature doesn't guarantee these benefits. A study published in *Scientific Reports* revealed that participants who walked in nature without their phones experienced notable reductions in stress, while those who brought their phones showed minimal improvement. Even the mere presence of an unused phone kept participants mentally tethered to daily distractions, diminishing nature's restorative effects. This highlights the importance of knowing when to leave technology behind.

Personally, my journeys to the Arctic have provided a profound escape precisely because they force me away from technology and noise. There's no phone service there, and no opportunity for distraction. The silence of the Arctic is unlike anything else on Earth. On those trips, I've spent hours, sometimes days, patiently waiting for storms to pass, sunsets and sunrises to slowly paint the sky, or the elusive Northern Lights to appear. These moments of complete silence and stillness profoundly impact me, revealing how deeply my mind craves quiet. Silence is an essential restorative state, a necessary pause that resets my mind and rejuvenates my body.

Another powerful way to restore mental balance is to allow ourselves to be bored. Today, boredom has virtually disappeared. Every spare moment instantly fills with screens, scrolling, or entertainment. Yet research increasingly points to boredom as crucial for creativity, insight, and mental rejuvenation. By intentionally reclaiming boredom and letting our minds wander without constant input, we can tap into deeper creativity and problem-solving skills.

Integrating these insights into daily life can dramatically transform how we feel:

- **Regularly disconnect:** Schedule deliberate periods each day to completely unplug from technology, even briefly.

- **Seek silence:** Intentionally spend time in quiet environments, fully present and free of distractions.

- **Embrace boredom:** Resist the urge to fill every idle moment. Allow space for your mind to wander, reflect, and recharge.

Restoring balance is about consciously creating space to step away, reclaiming the restorative quiet our ancestors naturally experienced.

Looking to the Horizon

One of the most powerful ways to prepare for an uncertain future is deliberately stepping outside of your comfort zone. While spending time reading or watching documentaries can be valuable, true growth comes from real, immersive experiences where the unfamiliar challenges you to adapt, learn, and evolve. The unknown is the greatest teacher.

My internship with Miss Universe was a whirlwind of profound lessons I could never have anticipated. Leaving behind my quiet small town in Ohio, I was thrown into bustling cities worldwide, navigating dense crowds, overcoming language barriers, and facing unexpected dangers head-on. Each experience tested and sharpened my adaptability, instincts, and resilience. Amid the chaos and uncertainty, what resonated most were the stark contrasts. I witnessed extreme poverty firsthand, seeing children in India sleeping directly on streets outside extravagant palaces. I visited hospitals through Aid for AIDS and worked alongside Children International in Mexico. Yet, even amid these harsh realities, I encountered some of the happiest and most generous people imaginable (Figure 16).

In Mexico, I met a family of six sharing one queen mattress on a dirt floor, with no running water or electricity. And honestly, they didn't seem to care. They laughed and smiled, their joy completely infectious. Watching them, it hit me hard: happiness isn't about what you have, but how you appreciate and experience life itself. Maybe happiness really is just a state of mind.

I also realized their happiness came from something deeper: the strength of their community. Their connections gave them purpose, meaning, and a sense of lasting happiness. They supported and encouraged each other through life's daily challenges. To me, happiness is deeply rooted in finding your tribe. In Blue Zones, strong community bonds were found to directly contribute to health, happiness, and longevity, proving just how powerful belonging and mutual support can be.

It's easy to lose sight of what's truly important, especially when modern life becomes overly complicated. Sometimes it's the simplest moments that carry the greatest meaning.

Figure 16: Panama and Mexico 2011, images by Erin E. Malone, Roston Ogata.

All of these experiences helped reshape my mindset and gave me the greatest gift: perspective. Perspective became the foundation of my resilience, clarifying what truly matters and helping me connect more deeply with my experiences and the world around me. I tap into this mindset when life feels overwhelming.

Today, I deliberately seek out new experiences, knowing each challenge expands my perspective, sharpens my skills, and deepens my adaptability. Sometimes, growth means embracing the unfamiliar.

I spent most of my twenties embarking on solo journeys, and while those experiences were deeply rewarding, I've found that sharing adventures with a partner adds a deeper sense of fulfillment. Having someone aligned with your goals, lifestyle, and passions significantly enriches the journey. My husband and I follow the same diet, maintain identical sleep schedules, and try to work out together as often as possible. We both love traveling and seeking new adventures, and having each other makes every step more meaningful and every challenge easier to navigate.

Mining Reward: Proof of Presence

Meaningful experiences like Bitcoin are finite, precious, and lasting. Disconnect, put down your phone, and fully engage. Moments mined intentionally today become priceless memories tomorrow.

Ikigai: Your Reason for Being

Beyond adding life to your years, longevity is about infusing those years with purpose and meaning. In Okinawa, residents embrace the concept of **Ikigai**, which translates roughly to "reason for being." Ikigai involves finding joy and purpose in everyday life. It's natural for your Ikigai to evolve throughout your life as your experiences and priorities shift.

Research consistently shows that having a clear sense of purpose strongly correlates with greater happiness, resilience, and longevity. When you pursue your Ikigai, you're also more likely to experience "**flow**," a state of complete immersion and focused engagement, often described as being "in the zone." This state contributes significantly to life satisfaction and overall well-being.

As you shape your future, reflect on your own Ikigai. Consider what genuinely fulfills you, inspires you, and connects you deeply to your community. A life guided by purpose is one you'll cherish and one that supports lasting health and well-being. Writing this book was absolutely a source of Ikigai for me.

The Future is Brighter Than You Think

When you think about your future, try to focus on possibilities instead of uncertainties. Imagine a world where chronic diseases become curable, clean energy is abundant for all, sustainable food systems thrive, and intelligent AI helps rebuild our foundational systems. Bitcoin restores honesty and accountability to money, allowing us to finally step off the financial hamster wheel driven by inflation and distorted incentives.

Visualize the extraordinary life possible when you actively prioritize your health, protect your sleep, cultivate a disciplined mindset, and secure your financial freedom through low-time-preference habits. Build resilience and adaptability through consistent effort, and seek out authentic and meaningful experiences.

I encourage you to intentionally embrace discomfort and commit to continuous learning. Approach each new experience with a beginner's mind; be open, curious, and ready to discover what you don't yet know. Prioritize your health today so you'll be ready to fully embrace tomorrow's breakthroughs. Manage your finances responsibly, so you're prepared to seize opportunities as they arise. The future isn't something to wait and hope for; it's something you actively create through each intentional choice you make.

Let this be your final challenge: share what you've learned with those around you. Share it with your family, your community, and your world. We are stronger when we lift each other up, and everyone deserves to thrive in the exciting future unfolding before us.

The future holds remarkable promise. Don't fear the unknown. Embrace what's ahead with curiosity, intention, and resilience.

Look to the horizon. The future is brighter than you think.

Afterword: The Journey Is Yours

Parts of this book have lived in my head for years. It's honestly surreal to see them finally come together, aligning in ways I could never have predicted. I've spent countless nights thinking about these ideas, refining them, testing them, and imagining how I might share them one day. Writing this book allowed me to revisit my own journey, reminding me why these principles became so important in the first place. It brought clarity to thoughts I've carried through countless conversations, meetups, and moments of reflection.

This process reaffirmed something important for me: these ideas become far more powerful through community, connection, and sharing them openly with others.

And that's where you come in. The journey doesn't end here. Join me at a Bitcoin meetup, connect online, or simply continue these conversations with your friends and family. The communities we build around these ideas make us stronger, more resilient, and better equipped to navigate whatever comes next.

The path forward belongs to you. Stay curious, keep questioning, and never settle for systems that hold you back. You have everything you need to future-proof your life.

Thank you for being part of this journey.

Glossary

Antifragility: The concept of benefiting and growing stronger from stress, volatility, and uncertainty rather than just enduring or surviving them. Antifragility is a proactive approach to life's inevitable challenges, turning obstacles into opportunities.

ASIC (Application-Specific Integrated Circuit): Computers designed for a single, specific purpose. In Bitcoin, ASICs are specifically optimized for mining by efficiently performing the computational task known as **hashing**.

Autophagy: A natural, internal cleaning process triggered primarily by fasting and caloric restriction, where the body clears damaged cells, regenerates healthier ones, and reduces inflammation.

Biological Age: A measurement assessing the true health and functionality of your body and cells, as opposed to chronological age (the number of years you've lived).

Biological Entropy: The gradual deterioration, aging, and loss of optimal function in biological systems, leading to increased health issues and reduced overall vitality.

Bitcoin: A decentralized, peer-to-peer form of money secured by cryptography, operating independently of banks or governments, enabling secure, transparent, and censorship-resistant financial transactions.

Bitcoin Miners: Refers either to the ASIC (Application-Specific Integrated Circuit) computer used for mining Bitcoin, or to the individual who operates such a device. Miners secure the Bitcoin network through **hashing,** and when successful, they add the next block to the blockchain, earning newly created bitcoin **(block subsidy)** and transaction fees.

Blockchain/Layer 1/ The Base Layer: Also referred to as the "timechain" by Satoshi, and commonly known as Layer 1 or the base chain. This decentralized, distributed ledger maintains a permanent record of every Bitcoin block mined since its inception. Each block, discovered approximately every 10 minutes, is timestamped and securely added to the chain, ensuring transparency, security, and immutability.

Block Subsidy: The amount of bitcoin a miner receives as a reward for successfully mining a block. This does not include bitcoin earned from transaction fees. Approximately every four years (or every 210,000 blocks), the block subsidy is cut in half, an event known as the halving, until eventually no new bitcoin will be created, capping Bitcoin's total supply at exactly 21 million coins.

Blue Zones: Geographical regions such as Okinawa (Japan), Sardinia (Italy), Nicoya (Costa Rica), Icaria (Greece), and Loma Linda (California), where residents consistently experience exceptional longevity and health. These areas are known for high concentrations of centenarians, people who live healthily to age 100 or older. Despite diverse geographies and cultures, Blue Zones share common lifestyle habits, including plant-rich diets, strong community bonds, consistent physical activity, and low stress levels, all of which significantly contribute to their remarkable longevity and overall well-being.

Cantillon Effect: A phenomenon where newly created money disproportionately benefits those who receive it first, typically large financial institutions, banks, and wealthy investors, allowing them to leverage easy credit to accumulate appreciating assets before inflation erodes its value for the broader population. It's a hidden advantage for the few at the expense of the many.

Chain Rollbacks: A controversial practice involving reversing or altering previously recorded transactions on a blockchain. This undermines trust and immutability, principles fundamental to decentralized systems, and is commonly done in altcoins. In Bitcoin, transactions are permanent and irreversible.

Circadian Rhythm: The body's natural internal clock regulates sleep-wake cycles, metabolism, and hormonal production, strongly influenced by daily exposure to natural light.

Cold Storage (Cold Wallet): A Bitcoin wallet storing private keys completely offline, typically using specialized hardware devices. Cold storage significantly reduces risks from hacking, malware, and online threats, offering greater security compared to internet-connected hot wallets.

Dollar Cost Averaging (DCA): An investment strategy where you invest a fixed amount of money at regular intervals, regardless of price fluctuations. This method smooths out volatility, removes emotional decision-making, and helps build a consistent, disciplined position over time, rather than attempting to time the market.

Dopamine: A neurotransmitter involved in reward, motivation, and pleasure, strongly influencing human behavior and habits. Managing dopamine through intentional actions can significantly enhance productivity and well-being.

Difficulty Adjustment: A mechanism built into the Bitcoin protocol to regulate the rate at which new blocks are added to the blockchain, ensuring one new block approximately every 10 minutes. The difficulty of mining Bitcoin is adjusted every 2016 blocks, or roughly every two weeks, based on the total computing power of the network. If miners collectively contribute more computing power, the difficulty increases to maintain the 10-minute block time. If computing power decreases, the difficulty decreases to maintain the same block time. This self-correcting mechanism helps ensure the stability, predictability, and security of the Bitcoin network.

Entropy: A universal measure of disorder, decay, and randomness within various systems, including biological health, financial stability, digital data integrity, and environmental sustainability.

Exahash: A unit equal to one quintillion hashes per second, used to measure computational power dedicated to Bitcoin mining.

The Federal Reserve (The Fed): The central banking system of the United States, established in 1913, responsible for monetary policy, financial stability, and managing inflation.

Fiat: Fiat refers to government-issued currency not backed by a physical commodity like gold or silver. Fiat's value primarily comes from the trust and faith people have in the issuing government. The term "fiat" means "by authoritative decree," derived from Latin for "let it be done," signifying the currency's value exists because the government declares it legal tender. Examples include the dollar, peso, lira, pound, euro, yuan, and yen.

Fixed Mindset: A belief that abilities and intelligence are largely predetermined or static. People with a fixed mindset view challenges as threats because they might expose perceived limitations, and often avoid growth opportunities due to fear of failure or inadequacy. This contrasts sharply with a **growth mindset**, which sees challenges as opportunities to learn and improve.

Flow State: A mental state of complete immersion and energized focus during an activity, enhancing productivity, creativity, and enjoyment.

Glymphatic System: A specialized waste-clearance pathway in the brain that actively flushes out harmful toxins and metabolic waste during deep, restorative sleep, helping to maintain neurological health and clarity.

Growth Mindset: Belief that personal abilities and intelligence can improve through effort and learning, in contrast to a fixed mindset, which views traits as predetermined and static.

Hara Hachi Bu: A Japanese practice from Okinawa, meaning "eat until you're 80% full." This mindful eating principle encourages stopping when no longer hungry, rather than eating until completely full, which supports longevity, metabolic health, and reduces the risk of chronic disease.

Hashing: The computational process used by Bitcoin miners, involving repeatedly guessing random, extremely large numbers until finding one below the network's specific **difficulty target**, a threshold that determines how challenging it is to mine a new block. This process secures transactions, validates new blocks, and maintains the integrity and security of the Bitcoin network.

Hashrate: The total computational power dedicated to mining and processing transactions on the Bitcoin network, a crucial indicator of network health, security, and mining activity.

Halving: A scheduled event approximately every four years (210,000 blocks), reducing the block subsidy reward miners receive by half, progressively decreasing the rate at which new bitcoin enters circulation until all 21 million bitcoin are mined around 2140.

Hardware Wallet: A physical device designed specifically to securely store private keys offline, typically resembling USB drives or small digital devices. Hardware wallets, the most common form of cold storage, generate seed words (typically 12 or 24 words) for secure backup and recovery, ensuring complete control over your assets.

Healthspan: The portion of life spent in good health, free from chronic diseases and functional decline, as opposed to simply lifespan, the total years lived.

Heart Rate Recovery (HRR): The measure of how quickly your heart rate returns to normal after intense exercise. HRR is an important indicator of cardiovascular health and autonomic nervous system adaptability. A higher HRR value (a greater drop in beats per minute) indicates better cardiovascular fitness and a more resilient nervous system.

Heart Rate Variability (HRV): A key biometric measuring the variation between consecutive heartbeats, reflecting the body's stress levels, adaptability, resilience, and overall cardiovascular health. Higher HRV typically indicates better stress management and recovery.

Heart Rate Zones: Specific ranges of heart rate measured as percentages of maximum heart rate, each corresponding to different exercise intensities and fitness goals, from fat burning and endurance training (Zone 2) to high-intensity performance (Zone 4 or 5).

High Time Preference: Prioritizing immediate gratification over long-term gains, often resulting in decisions negatively impacting long-term health, wealth, and stability.

HODL: Originating from a 2013 Bitcoin forum typo ("I AM HOD-LING"), HODL has become a rallying cry and mindset within the Bitcoin community. It signals you've done the work, understand Bitcoin's value, and aren't selling due to short-term market fluctuations. You're committed to the long-term vision, actively prioritizing low time preference and disciplined financial decision-making.

Hormesis: A biological concept where low-to-moderate stress exposure, such as exercise, fasting, sauna, or cold exposure, stimulates beneficial adaptations, improving health and resilience.

Hot Wallet: A Bitcoin wallet connected directly to the internet, such as smartphone or computer applications. Hot wallets offer convenience and ease of use for everyday transactions but come with higher risks due to online vulnerabilities like hacking or malware, compared to offline storage methods such as cold wallets.

Hyperinflation: An extreme economic condition marked by rapid, uncontrollable price increases due to excessive money printing, severely eroding currency value and purchasing power.

Ikigai: A Japanese concept translating to "reason for being," embodying finding deep joy, purpose, and fulfillment in everyday life activities, significantly contributing to longevity and satisfaction.

Lightning Network: A decentralized, trustless, second-layer payment solution built directly on Bitcoin's base blockchain (Layer 1), enabling instant, nearly free, scalable transactions.

Longevity: The proactive pursuit of extending both lifespan and healthspan through intentional lifestyle habits, nutrition, exercise, and emerging scientific advances.

Low Time Preference: Prioritizing long-term rewards over immediate pleasures, promoting disciplined financial choices, sustainable health habits, and thoughtful lifestyle decisions.

Melatonin: A hormone produced by the pineal gland, essential for regulating sleep-wake cycles and circadian rhythms, strongly influenced by exposure to natural and artificial light.

Microgrid: A small-scale, localized power network operating independently from the main electrical grid, delivering electricity directly to isolated communities or remote locations.

Mining (Bitcoin): The computational proof-of-work process validating Bitcoin transactions, adding them to the blockchain, and rewarding miners with newly minted bitcoin (block subsidy) and transaction fees.

Mining Pool: A collective group of Bitcoin miners who combine computational power to increase the chance of mining a block, distributing rewards more consistently.

Multisignature (Multisig): A wallet setup requiring multiple private keys to authorize transactions; for example, needing 2 out of 3 keys. Multisig significantly increases security, reducing the risk of loss or theft by eliminating any single point of failure, making it more secure than a single-signature wallet.

Nostr: A decentralized, open-source social media protocol integrating directly with the Bitcoin Lightning Network, enabling censorship-resistant communication and direct financial transactions between users.

Personal Sovereignty: Taking full ownership and control of one's financial, physical, and mental well-being, independent from reliance on external institutions or authorities.

Pre-Mines: A controversial practice, commonly done in altcoins, where developers allocate a significant amount of cryptocurrency tokens to themselves before releasing them to the public. Pre-mines are often criticized for creating centralized control, unfair advantages, and reducing transparency and trust within the project.

Proof of Work (PoW): In Bitcoin, miners secure the network through computational power by repeatedly guessing random, extremely large numbers in a process known as **hashing**, validating transactions to earn rewards. In life, proof of work represents earning valuable outcomes through genuine effort, discipline, and sacrifice.

Reactive Healthcare: A healthcare model addressing symptoms and diseases only after they manifest, rather than proactively identifying and preventing underlying causes.

Resting Heart Rate (RHR): The number of heartbeats per minute while at rest, an essential indicator of cardiovascular fitness and overall health.

Satoshi (Sats): The smallest unit of bitcoin. One bitcoin is divisible into 100 million satoshis, often called "sats." People typically accumulate bitcoin by regularly "stacking sats," gradually and practically building their holdings without needing to buy an entire bitcoin at once.

Satoshi Nakamoto: The pseudonymous creator(s) of Bitcoin, who authored its original white paper, created the protocol, and launched the world's first decentralized, peer-to-peer form of money, governed purely by mathematics and code rather than centralized institutions. Satoshi's innovation solved long-standing problems of trust, centralization, and financial control, introducing scarcity and transparency to money. To this day, Satoshi's true identity remains unknown, further emphasizing Bitcoin's neutrality and decentralization.

Seed Words: A sequence of typically 12 or 24 words generated by Bitcoin wallets, providing a secure backup and recovery method to maintain complete control over Bitcoin holdings.

Self-Custody: Independently controlling and safeguarding one's own Bitcoin or assets, ensuring personal sovereignty through secure private key management. In health, self-custody involves proactively managing personal well-being by questioning conventional wisdom, deliberate experimentation, data tracking, and relentless self-advocacy.

Shinrin-Yoku (Forest Bathing): The Japanese practice of "forest bathing," which involves mindful immersion in natural forest environments, has been scientifically proven to reduce stress, lower blood pressure, and enhance immune function.

Single Signature (Single-Sig): A wallet setup requiring just one private key to authorize transactions. While simpler and convenient, single-sig wallets carry higher risks compared to **multisignature** wallets, due to the single point of failure if the private key is lost or compromised.

Sleep Apnea: A potentially serious sleep disorder characterized by repeated interruptions in breathing during sleep, severely impacting sleep quality and overall health.

Stranded Energy: Energy produced in remote areas far from electrical grids or populations, unused because transmitting it to populated areas is not cost-effective or technically feasible.

VO$_2$ Max: Maximum rate of oxygen consumption measured during incremental exercise, a key indicator of cardiovascular fitness, endurance, and overall health.

References by Chapter

All sources accessed between March and July 2025. Sources for all tables and figures in this book are included in the references below.

Chapter 2:

"A Blueprint for Bitcoin Mining and Energy in Africa." *Gridless Compute*, May 17, 2023. https://gridlesscompute.com/2023/05/17/a-blue print-for-bitcoin-mining-and-energy-in-africa/.

Adejumobi, Oluwapelumi. "Marathon Digital Warms 80,000 Finnish Homes with Heat Generated from Bitcoin Mining." *CryptoSlate*, December 20, 2023. https://cryptoslate.com/marathon-digital-warms-80000-finnish-homes-with-heat-generated-from-bitcoin-mining/.

Back, Adam. "Hashcash – A Denial of Service Counter-Measure." August 1, 2002. https://sites.cs.ucsb.edu/~rich/class/old.cs290/papers/has cash2.pdf.

"Bitcoin Mining and District Heating: A Match Made in Heaven." *NiceHash*, March 17, 2025. https://www.nicehash.com/blog/post/bit coin-mining-and-district-heating-a-match-made-in-heaven.

District Energy. "Finland's Households Turn to Bitcoin Mining to Heat Homes." *District Energy*, April 25, 2024. https://www.districtener gy.org/blogs/district-energy/2024/04/25/finlands-households-turn-to-bitcoin-mining-to-heat.

Dwork, Cynthia, and Moni Naor. "Pricing via Processing or Combatting Junk Mail." *Weizmann Institute of Science,* 1992. https://www.wis dom.weizmann.ac.il/~naor/PAPERS/pvp.pdf.

Redman, Jamie. "Riot Showcases Demand Response Strategy: Bitcoin Mining's Role in Strengthening Texas Energy Grid." *Bitcoin.com News*, September 7, 2023. https://news.bitcoin.com/riot-showcases-de mand-response-strategy-bitcoin-minings-role-in-strengthening-tex as-energy-grid.

"SDG7: Data and Projections – Access to Electricity." *International Energy Agency*, 2024. https://www.iea.org/reports/sdg7-data-and-projec tions/access-to-electricity.

Vu, Kevin and Emily Foxhall. "Texas Bitcoin Profit: How Bitcoin Mining Became a Boon for the State's Electricity Market." *Texas Tribune*, January 3, 2024. https://www.texastribune.org/2024/01/03/tex as-bitcoin-profit-electricity/.

Chapter 3:

Albright, Haley, Paul S. Riehl, Christopher C. McAtee, et al. "Catalytic Carbonyl-Olefin Metathesis of Aliphatic Ketones: Iron(III) Homo-Dimers as Lewis Acidic Superelectrophiles." *ACS Catalysis* 9, no. 6 (2019): 5620–5627. https://pmc.ncbi.nlm.nih. gov/articles/PMC6532644/.

Brown University Health Blog Team. "How to Live to 100: Lessons from Italy." *Brown University Health*, July 27, 2023. https://www.brown health.org/be-well/how-live-100-lessons-italy.

Clausen, Johan S.R., Jacob L. Marott, et al. "Midlife Cardiorespiratory Fitness and the Long-Term Risk of Mortality: 46 Years of Follow-Up." *Journal of the American College of Cardiology* 72, no. 9 (2018): 987–995. https://pubmed.ncbi.nlm.nih.gov/30139444/.

Clear, James. "How to Build a New Habit: This is Your Strategy Guide." *James Clear*. https://jamesclear.com/habit-guide.

Daugherty, Greg. "What is Quiet Quitting—and Is It a Real Thing?" *Investopedia,* October 8, 2024. https://www.investopedia.com/ what-is-quiet-quitting-6743910.

Johnson, Bryan. "What is HRR, and How to Improve It." *Blueprint*, December 11, 2024. https://blueprint.bryanjohnson.com/blogs/ news/how-to-improve-your-heart-rate-recovery.

"Live to 100: Secrets of the Blue Zones." *Netflix*, directed by Clay Jeter, MakeMake Entertainment, 2023.

"NVSS - Life Expectancy." *CDC National Center for Health Statistics*, April 8, 2025. https://www.cdc.gov/nchs/nvss/life-expectancy.htm.

O'Brien, Ellen. "What's Your VO2 Max? The Answer Could Transform Your Health." *National Geographic*, August 7, 2024. https://www.nationalgeographic.com/science/article/vo2-max-explained.

Quinn, Elizabeth. "Using the Cooper Test 12-Minute Run to Check Aerobic Fitness." *Verywell Fit*. Updated on April 25, 2024. https://www.verywellfit.com/fitness-test-for-endurance-12-minute-run-3120264.

Rakshit, Shameek and Matthew McGough. "How Does U.S. Life Expectancy Compare to Other Countries?" *Peterson-KFF Health System Tracker*, February 14, 2025. https://www.healthsystemtracker.org/chart-collection/u-s-life-expectancy-compare-countries/.

"What's a Good VO2 Max for Me? Your Aerobic Fitness Explained" *Garmin*, July 12, 2022. https://www.garmin.com/en-US/blog/fitness/whats-a-good-vo2-max-for-me/.

Chapter 4:

"Average Sales Price of Houses Sold for the United States." *Federal Reserve Bank of St. Louis*, April 23, 2025. https://fred.stlouisfed.org/series/ASPUS.

"Bitcoin Price Chart By Month 2016." *StatMuse Money*. https://www.statmuse.com/money/ask/bitcoin-price-chart-by-month-2016.

"Bitcoin Price Chart By Month 2020." *StatMuse Money*. https://www.statmuse.com/money/ask/bitcoin-price-chart-by-month-2020.

"Bitcoin Price Chart By Month 2024." *StatMuse Money*. https://www.statmuse.com/money/ask/bitcoin-price-chart-by-month-2024.

"Consumer Price Index for All Urban Consumers: Purchasing Power of the Consumer Dollar in U.S. City Average." *Federal Reserve Bank of St. Louis*, June 11, 2025. https://fred.stlouisfed.org/series/CUUR0000SA0R.

Chapter 5:

American Society for Nutrition. "Most People Think Their Diet Is Healthier Than It Is." June 14, 2022. https://nutrition.org/most-people-think-their-diet-is-healthier-than-it-is/.

American College of Sports Medicine. *ACSM's Guidelines for Exercise Testing and Prescription*, 11th ed. Wolters Kluwer, 2022.

Anastasiou, C.A., M. Yannakoulia, M.H. Kosmidis, et al. "Mediterranean Diet and Cognitive Health: Initial Results from the Hellenic Longitudinal Investigation of Ageing and Diet." *PLOS ONE, 12*(8), 2017. https://doi.org/10.1371/journal.pone.0182048.

Anderson, Kate (ed.). "Ultra-Processed Foods Cause Overeating and Weight Gain, NIH Study Finds." *News-Medical.net*, May 16, 2019. https://www.news-medical.net/news/20190516/Ultra-processed-foods-cause-overeating-and-weight-gain-NIH-study-finds.aspx.

Azaza M.S., S.A. Saidi, M.N. Dhraief, and A. El-Feki. "Growth Performance, Nutrient Digestibility, Hematological Parameters, and Hepatic Oxidative Stress Response in Juvenile Nile Tilapia, *Oreochromis niloticus*, Fed Carbohydrates of Different Complexities." *Animals (Basel)*, 10(10), October 19, 2020. https://doi.org/10.3390/ani10101913.

"Blue Zones." *BlueZones.com*. https://www.bluezones.com/.

Brown, R.E., K.L. Canning, M. Fung, et al. "Calorie Estimation in Adults Differing in Body Weight Class and Weight Loss Status." *Medicine and Science in Sports and Exercise, 48(3), 521–526, 2016*. https://doi.org/10.1249/MSS.0000000000000796.

Castle, L., M. Andreassen, G. Aquilina, et al. "Re-evaluation of Pullulan (E 1204) as a FoodAdditive and New Application for its Extension of Use." *EFSA Journal, 23*(3), 2023. https://doi.org/10.2903/j.efsa.2025.9267.

Cena, Hellas and Philip C. Calder. "Defining a Healthy Diet: Evidence for the Role of Contemporary Dietary Patterns in Health and Disease." *Nutrients*, 12(2), January 27, 2020. https://doi.org/10.3390/nu12020334.

Centers for Disease Control and Prevention. "Almost Half of Americans Use at Least One Prescription Drug: Annual Report on Nation's Health Shows." *National Center for Health Statistics*, December 2, 2004. https://www.cdc.gov/nchs/pressroom/04news/hus04.htm.

Centers for Disease Control and Prevention. "Adult Obesity Facts." *CDC. gov*, May 14, 2024. https://www.cdc.gov/obesity/adult-obesity-facts.

Centers for Disease Control and Prevention. "Antimicrobial Resistance Facts and Stats." *CDC.gov*, February 4, 2025. https://www.cdc.gov/anti biotic-use/antimicrobial-resistance.html.

Centers for Disease Control and Prevention. "COVID-19: U.S. Impact on Antimicrobial Resistance, Special Report 2022." *U.S. Department of Health and Human Services*, 2022. https://www.cdc.gov/drugre sistance/covid19.html.

Centers for Disease Control and Prevention. "Life Expectancy in the U.S. Dropped for the Second Year in a Row in 2021." *National Center for Health Statistics*, August 31, 2022. https://www.cdc.gov/nchs/ pressroom/nchs_press_releases/2022/20220831.htm.

Centers for Disease Control and Prevention. "STEADI: Stopping Elderly Accidents, Deaths & Injuries – 30-Second Chair Stand Assessment." *CDC.gov*, 2017. https://www.cdc.gov/steadi.

Debras, Charlotte, Eloi Chazelas, Bernard Srour, et al. "Artificial Sweeteners and Cancer Risk: Results from the NutriNet-Santé Population-Based Cohort Study." *PLOS Medicine,* 19(3), March 24, 2022. https://doi.org/10.1371/journal.pmed.1003950.

"Diet and Dementia: Foods That Increase or Decrease Alzheimer's Risk." *BlueZones.com.* https://www.bluezones.com/2017/07/diet-de mentia-foods-increase-decrease-alzheimers-risk.

Elbel, Brian. "Consumer Estimation of Recommended and Actual Calories at Fast Food Restaurants." *Obesity (Silver Spring),* 21(7), 1362–1369, 2013. https://doi.org/10.1002/oby.20308.

Endocrine Society. "Study Finds Over 80 percent of COVID-19 Patients Have Vitamin D Deficiency." *Endocrine*, October 27, 2020. https:// www.endocrine.org/news-and-advocacy/news-room/2020/study-finds-over-80-percent-of-covid19-patients-have-vitamin-d-deficiency.

Fangmeyer, Jens, Arne Behrens, and Barabara Gleede et al. "Mass-Spectrometric Imaging of Electrode Surfaces—a View on Electrochemical Side Reactions." *PMC PubMed Central*, September 2, 2020. https://pmc.ncbi.nlm.nih.gov/articles/PMC7693111/.

"Feed-to-Meat Conversion Inefficiency Ratios." *A Well-Fed World*, October 26, 2015. https://awellfedworld.org/feedratios.

Food and Drug Administration. "FDA to Revoke Authorization for Use of Red No. 3 in Food and Ingested Drugs." *U.S. Food and Drug Administration*, January 15, 2025. https://www.fda.gov/food/hfp-constituent-updates/fda-revoke-authorization-use-red-no-3-food-and-ingested-drugs.

Hales, C.M., M.D. Carroll, C.D. Fryar, and C.L. Ogden. "Prevalence of Obesity and Severe Obesity Among Adults: United States, 2017–2018." NCHS Data Brief, no. 360. *National Center for Health Statistics*, 2020. https://www.cdc.gov/nchs/products/databriefs/db360.htm.

Hall, Kevin, Alexis Ayuketah, and Robert Brychta et al. "Ultra-Processed Diets Cause Excess Calorie Intake and Weight Gain: An Inpatient Randomized Controlled Trial of Ad Libitum Food Intake. *PMC PubMed Central*, March 10, 2021. https://pmc.ncbi.nlm.nih.gov/articles/PMC7946062/.

IARC. "Monograph Volume 112-1." *International Agency for Research on Cancer*, July 2018. https://www.iarc.who.int/wp-content/uploads/2018/07/MonographVolume112-1.pdf.

Johnson, Bryan. (2025). *Why You Need Data: Test your biological age for $0. YouTube.* https://www.youtube.com/watch?v=veJzV8iA6gg.

Kaiser Family Foundation. "Prescription Drug Trends—A Chartbook." kff.org, 2020. https://www.kff.org/health-costs/issue-brief/prescription-drug-trends-chartbook/.

Kaiser Family Foundation. "Retail Prescription Drugs Filled at Pharmacies per Capita." kff.org, 2020. https://www.kff.org/health-costs/state-indicator/retail-rx-drugs-per-capita/.

Li, Y., Y. Li, X. Gu, et al. "Long-Term Intake of Red Meat in Relation to Dementia Risk and Cognitive Function in US Adults." *Neurology*, 104(3). 2025. https://doi.org/10.1212/WNL.0000000000208861.

Martínez, Steele E, LG Baraldi, ML Louzada, et al. "Ultra-processed Foods and Added Sugars in the US Diet: Evidence from a Nationally Representative Cross-Sectional Study." *BMJ Open* 6(3):e009892, 2016. doi: 10.1136/bmjopen-2015-009892.

Massy-Westropp, N.M., T.K. Gill, A.W. Taylor, R.W. Bohannon, and C.L. Hill. "Hand Grip Strength: Age and Gender Stratified Normative Data in a Population-Based Study." *BMC Research Notes*, 4:127, 2011. https://doi.org/10.1186/1756-0500-4-127.

Mayo Clinic. "How Fit Are You? See How You Measure Up." *Mayo Clinic*, 2024. https://www.mayoclinic.org/healthy-lifestyle/fitness/in-depth/how-fit-are-you/art-20463847.

Mialon, Mélissa, Paulo Matos Serodio, and Eric Crosbie et al. "Conflicts of Interest for Members of the US 2020 Dietary Guidelines Advisory Committee." *Public Health Nutrition*, 27(1):69–80, 2024. https://doi.org/10.1017/S1368980022000672.

Mykyta, L., and R.A. Cohen, "Characteristics of Adults Aged 18–64 Who Did Not Take Medication as Prescribed to Reduce Costs: United States, 2021." NCHS Data Brief, No. 470. *National Center for Health Statistics*, 2023. https://www.cdc.gov/nchs/products/data briefs/db470.htm.

"National Health Expenditures 2023: Health Care Spending in the US Reached $4.9 Trillion and Increased 7.5 percent in 2023." *Health Affairs,* December 18, 2024. https://doi.org/10.1377/hlthaff.2024.01375.

NCD Risk Factor Collaboration (NCD-RisC). "Worldwide Trends in Diabetes Since 1980: A Pooled Analysis of 751 Population-Based Studies with 4.4 Million Participants." *The Lancet*, 387(10027): 1513-1530, 2016. https://doi.org/10.1016/S0140-6736(16)00618-8.

Lichtman, S.W., K. Pisarska, E.R. Berman, et al. "Discrepancy between Self-Reported and Actual Caloric Intake and Exercise in Obese

Subjects." New England Journal of Medicine, 327(27), 1893–1898, 1992. https://doi.org/10.1056/NEJM199212313272701.

Neslen, A. "FAO Draft Report Backs Growth of Livestock Industry Despite Emissions." *Climate Home News*, 2024. https://www.climatechange news.com/2024/08/14/fao-draft-report-backs-growth-of-livestock-industry-despite-emissions.

Nevill, A.M., G.R. Tomkinson, J.J.Lang, and W. Wutz. "How Should Adult Handgrip Strength Be Normalized? Allometry Reveals New Insights and Associated Reference Curves." *Medicine & Science in Sports & Exercise*, 54(1), 162-168, 2022. https://doi.org/10.1249/MSS.0000000000002751.

Nielsen, N.M., T.G. Junker, S.G. Boelt, et al. "Vitamin D Status and Severity of COVID-19." *Scientific Reports* 12, 19823 (2022). https://doi.org/10.1038/s41598-022-21513-9.

O'Neill, J. "Tackling Drug-Resistant Infections Globally: Final Report and Recommendations." *Review on Antimicrobial Resistance*, 2016. https://amr-review.org/sites/default/files/160525_Final%20paper_with%20cover.pdf.

Our World in Data. "Agricultural Land by Global Diets." *OurWorldInData. org.* https://ourworldindata.org/agricultural-land-by-global-diets.

Our World in Data. "Land Use by Diets." *OurWorldInData.org.* https://our worldindata.org/land-use-diets.

Patterson, Daniel J. "Vegetable Oils: A History of Fats Gone Wrong." *Zero Acre Farms*, April 9, 2023. https://www.zeroacre.com/blog/the-history-of-vegetable-oils.

Qiu, Y., W. Bao, X. Tian, et al. "Vitamin D Status in Hospitalized COVID-19 Patients is Associated with Disease Severity and IL-5 Production." *Virology Journal* 20, 212, 2023. https://doi.org/10.1186/s12985-023-02165-1.

Reynolds A, J. Mann, J. Cummings, N. Winter, et al. "Carbohydrate Quality and Human Health: A Series of Systematic Reviews and Meta-Analyses." *Lancet*, 393(10170):434-445, 2019 https://doi.org/10.1016/S0140-6736(18)31809-9.

Ritchie, Hannah. "Food Production is Responsible for One-Quarter of the World's Greenhouse Gas Emissions" *OurWorldinData.org*, 2019. https://ourworldindata.org/food-ghg-emissions.

Sifferlin, Alexandra. "Soda Companies Fund 96 Health Groups in the U.S." *Time.com*, October 10, 2016. https://time.com/4522940/soda-pepsi-coke-health-obesity.

U.S. Centers for Medicare & Medicaid Services. "National Health Expenditure Data." *CMS.gov*, 2024. https://www.cms.gov/data-research/statistics-trends-and-reports/national-health-expenditure-data.

USDA Economic Research Service. "ERS Data Series Tracks Major Uses of U.S. Land with a Focus on Agriculture." *Amber Waves*, December 2024. https://www.ers.usda.gov/amber-waves/2024/december/ers-data-series-tracks-major-uses-of-u-s-land-with-a-focus-on-agriculture.

U.S. Department of Agriculture, Economic Research Service. "Soybeans and Oil Crops - Related data & Statistics." *USDA*, January 8, 2025. https://www.ers.usda.gov/topics/crops/soybeans-and-oil-crops/related-data-statistics.

U.S. Department of Health and Human Services. "Background on Obesity - The Surgeon General's Vision for a Healthy and Fit Nation." *National Library of Medicine.* https://www.ncbi.nlm.nih.gov/books/NBK44656.

Vogel, Kaitlin. "A Chemical Found in Common Artificial Sweetener May Cause DNA Damage, Cancer." *Medical News Today,* July 17, 2023. https://www.medicalnewstoday.com/articles/a-chemical-found-in-common-artificial-sweetener-may-cause-dna-damage-cancer.

Wager, Emma, Matthew McGough, Shameek Rakshit, et al. "How Does Health Spending in the U.S. Compare to Other Countries?" Peterson-KFF Health System Tracker, April 19, 2025. https://www.healthsystemtracker.org/chart-collection/health-spending-u-s-compare-countries.

Wallinga, D., E. Klein, and A. Hamilton. "U.S. Livestock Antibiotic Use is Rising, Medical Use Falls." *Natural Resources Defense Council,*

2021. https://www.nrdc.org/experts/david-wallinga/us-livestock-antibiotic-use-rising-medical-use-falls.

Willcox D.C., B.J. Willcox, H. Todoriki, and M. Suzuki "The Okinawan Diet: Health Implications of a Low-Calorie, Nutrient-Dense, Antioxidant-Rich Dietary Pattern Low in Glycemic Load." *Journal of the American College of Nutrition*, 28 Suppl 4, 500S–516S, 2009. https://doi.org/10.1080/07315724.2009.10718117.

World Bank. "Life Expectancy at Birth, Total (Years) - United States." *World Bank*. https://data.worldbank.org/indicator/SP.DYN.LE00. IN?locations=US.

Chapter 6:

ABC News. "What Science Says About the Best Time of Day to Break an Olympic Record." August 10, 2016. https://abcnews.go.com.

Lee, I.H., and S.Y. Park. "Balance Improvement by Strength Training for the Elderly." *The Journal of Physical Therapy Science 25(12), 1591–1593, 2013. https://doi.org/10.1589/jpts.25.1591.*

Lima, N. C., R. Kirovand K.M. de Almondes, "Impairment of Executive Functions Due to Sleep Alterations: An Integrative Review on the Use of Event-Related Potentials." *Frontiers in Neuroscience*, 16, 2022. https://doi.org/10.3389/fnins.2022.906492.

National Institutes of Health. "Sleep Deprivation Increases Alzheimer's Protein." *NIH Research Matters*, 2018. https://www.nih.gov/news-events/news-releases/sleep-deprivation-increases-alzheimers-protein.

Ruhl, C. " 5 Stages Of Sleep (REM And Non-REM Sleep Cycles)." *Simply Psychology*. 2023. https://www.simplypsychology.org/sleep-stages.html.

Suni, E. " How Lack of Sleep Impacts Cognitive Performance and Focus." *Sleep Foundation*, 2023. https://www.sleepfoundation.org/sleep-deprivation/lack-of-sleep-and-cognitive-impairment.

Vanderbilt University School of Medicine. "MPH's Diamond: Late afternoon, Early Evening Best Time of Day to Break Olympic Records." *Vanderbilt University*, 2016. https://medschool.vander

bilt.edu/mph/2016/08/11/mphs-diamond-late-afternoon-early-evening-best-time-of-day-to-break-olympic-records/.

Viola-Saltzman, M., and N.F. Watson. "Traumatic Brain Injury and Sleep Disorders." *Neurologic Clinics*, (4):1299-312, 2012. https://doi.org/10.1016/j.ncl.2012.08.008.

Walker, Matthew. *Why We Sleep*, 2017.

Werner, J.K., J. Albrecht, V.F. Capaldi et al. "Association of Biomarkers of Neuronal Injury and Inflammation With Insomnia Trajectories After Traumatic Brain Injury: A TRACK-TBI Study." *Neurology* 102(8), 2024. https://doi.org/10.1212/WNL.0000000000209269.

Chapter 7

"Average Daily Time Spent Watching TV per Capita in the United States from 2009 to 2023, by age Group (In Hours)." *Statista*. https://www.statista.com/statistics/411775/average-daily-time-watching-tv-us-by-age/.

Bitcoin Visuals. "Lightning Network Capacity." *Bitcoin Visuals*. https://bitcoinvisuals.com/ln-capacity.

Boulares, A., H. Jdidi, and W. Douzi. "Cold and Longevity: Can Cold Exposure Counteract Aging?" Life Sciences, 364, 2025. https://doi.org/10.1016/j.lfs.2025.123431.

Cha, H, M.P. Farina, C.T. Chiu, and M.D. Hayward. "The Importance of Education for Understanding Variability of Dementia Onset in the United States." *Demographic Research* 50:733-762, 2024. https://doi.org/10.4054/demres.2024.50.26.

Carter, Nic. "Go West, Bitcoin! Unpacking the Great Hashrate Migration." *CoinDesk,* 2022, https://www.coindesk.com/policy/2021/06/22/go-west-bitcoin-unpacking-the-great-hashrate-migration.

Draaisma, D. *Why Life Speeds Up As You Get Older: How Memory Shapes Our Past.* Cambridge University Press, 2016.

Avni-Babad, Dinah, and Ilana Ritov. "Routine and the Perception of Time." Journal of Experimental Psychology, 32(6), 543–550, Dec. 2003. https://pubmed.ncbi.nlm.nih.gov/14640847/.

Duarte, F. "Alarming Average Screen Time Statistics." *Exploding Topics.* https://explodingtopics.com/blog/screen-time-stats.

Fitzgerald, Toni. "Americans Are Watching Less TV As Prices Rise, Study Suggests." *Forbes*, July 16, 2024. https://www.forbes.com/sites/ton ifitzgerald/2024/07/16/study-americans-are-watching-less-and-less-tv-heres-why/.

James, William. *The Principles of Psychology.* Henry Holt and Company, 1890.

Johns Hopkins Hospital. "Does Higher Learning Combat Dementia?" *Johns Hopkins Medicine.* https://www.hopkinsmedicine.org/health/well ness-and-prevention/does-higher-learning-combat-dementia.

Mayo Clinic. "Stress Management." *Mayo Clinic*, Nov. 21, 2023. https:// www.mayoclinic.org/healthy-lifestyle/stress-management/in-depth/ positive-thinking/art-20043950.

Primeau, Mia. "Your Powerful, Changeable Mindset." *Stanford Report,* September 15th, 2021. https://news.stanford.edu/stories/2021/09/ mindsets-clearing-lens-life.

Schultz, W. "Dopamine Reward Prediction-Error Signalling: A Two-Component Response." *Nature Reviews Neuroscience*, 17(3), 183–195, 2016.

"Share of Consumers Watching Television on a Daily Basis in the United States from 2022 to 2024" *Statista.* https://www.statista. com/statistics/1490432/consumers-watch-tv-per-day-us/.

Taleb, N.N. *Antifragile: Things That Gain from Disorder.* Random House, 2012.

Voss, P., M.E. Thomas, J.M. Cisneros-Franco, and É. de Villers-Sidani, "Dynamic Brains and the Changing Rules of Neuroplasticity: Implications for Learning and Recovery." *Frontiers in Psychology*, 8, 1657, 2017.

Wittmann, M., and S. Lehnhoff. "Age Effects in Perception of Time." *Psychological Reports*, 97(3), 921-935, 2005.

Zakay, D. "Experiencing Time in Daily Life." *Psychology of Time*, pp. 219-240, 2012.

Chapter 8:

IQAir. "New EPA Annual PM2.5 Air Quality Standards Expected to Save Lives." *iQAir,* 2024. https://www.iqair.com/us/newsroom/new-epa-annual-pm25-air-quality-standards-expected-save-lives.

"Landfill Methane Regulations Workshop." *California Air Resources Board,* May 18, 2023. https://ww2.arb.ca.gov.

Volcovici, Valerie. "Aerial Surveys Show US Landfills are Major Source of Methane Emissions." *Reuters,* March 28, 2024. https://www.reuters.com/world/us/aerial-surveys-show-us-landfills-are-major-source-methane-emissions-2024-03-28/.

Chapter 9:

King, Dominic & Harsha Nori. "The Path to Medical Superintelligence." *Microsoft AI*, June 30, 2025. https://microsoft.ai/new/the-path-to-medical-superintelligence/?utm_source=chatgpt.com.

Knight, Will. "Microsoft Says Its New AI System Diagnosed Patients 4 Times More Accurately Than Human Doctors." *Wired,* Jun 30, 2025. https://www.wired.com/story/microsoft-medical-superintelligence-diagnosis/.

Pesheva, Ekaterina. "A New Artificial Intelligence Tool for Cancer." *Harvard Medical School*, September 2, 2024. https://hms.harvard.edu/news/new-artificial-intelligence-tool-cancer.

SBG TV (ABC). "AI in Medicine: Beware of Misdiagnosis." *ABC HQHA*, March 7th 2025. https://khqa.com/sponsored/spotlight/ai-in-medicine-beware-of-misdiagnosis.

Tyson, Alec, Giancarlo Pasquini, Alison Spencer, and Cary Funk. "60% of Americans Would Be Uncomfortable With Provider Relying on AI in Their Own Health Care." *Pew Research Center*, February 22, 2023. https://www.pewresearch.org/science/2023/02/22/60-of-americans-would-be-uncomfortable-with-provider-relying-on-ai-in-their-own-health-care/.

Whelan, Sarah. "AI Model May Help Guide Cancer Diagnosis and Treatment." *Technology Networks Cancer Research*, September 9,

2024. https://www.technologynetworks.com/cancer-research/news/ai-model-may-help-guide-cancer-diagnosis-and-treatment-390679.

Chapter 10:

Brown, Susan. "Forest Bathing: Healing in Nature." *Better Bones*, 2016. https://betterbones.com/the-natural-approach/forest-bathing-healing-in-nature/.

Cohen, R., C. Bavishi, and A. Rozanski. "Purpose in Life and Its Relationship to All-Cause Mortality and Cardiovascular Events: A Meta-Analysis." Psychosomatic Medicine, 78(2), 122–133, 2016. https://doi.org/10.1097/PSY.0000000000000274.

"The Dangers of Sitting: Why Sitting is the New Smoking." *Better Health*. https://www.betterhealth.vic.gov.au/health/healthyliving/the-dangers-of-sitting.

Gaines, Jeffrey. "The Philosophy of Ikigai: 3 Examples About Finding Purpose." *Positive Psychology*, May 13, 2025. https://positivepsychology.com/ikigai.

Kotifani, Aislinn. "Research Says Walking This Much Per Week Extends Your Life." *Blue Zones*. https://www.bluezones.com/2018/07/research-says-walking-this-much-per-week-extends-your-life/.

Koop, Katy. "Evolutionary Biologist: Our Hunter-Gatherer Past and the Exercise-Brain Health Link." *Being Patient*, July 14, 2024. https://www.beingpatient.com/david-raichlen-exercise-brain-health-human-evolution.

O'Keefe, E.L. and C. J. Lavie. "A Hunter-Gatherer Exercise Prescription to Optimize Health and Well-Being in the Modern World." *Progress in Cardiovascular Diseases*, 64:77–82, 2021. https://doi.org/10.1016/j.pcad.2020.12.003.

Pate, R.R., M. O'Neill, and S.N. Blair. "Sedentary Behaviors Increase Risk of Cardiovascular Disease Mortality in Men: The Aerobics Center Longitudinal Study." *Medicine & Science in Sports & Exercise*, 38(Suppl), S666–S667, 2006. https://doi.org/10.1249/00005768-200605001-02829.

Sayre, M.K., M. Anyawire, B.M. Wood, H. Pontzer, and D.A. Raichlen. "Lifestyle and Patterns of Physical Activity in Hadza Foragers." American Journal of Biological Anthropology, 182(3), 340–356, 2023. https://doi.org/10.1002/ajpa.24846.

Siah C.J.R., Y.S. Goh YS, J. Lee J, et al. "The Effects of Forest Bathing on Psychological Well-Being: A Systematic Review and Meta-Analysis." *International Journal of Mental Health Nursing* 32(4), 1038–1054, 2023. https://doi.org/10.1111/inm.13131.

www.ingramcontent.com/pod-product-compliance
Lightning Source LLC
Chambersburg PA
CBHW062051270326
41931CB00013B/3028